Fail-Safe Strategies for Science and Literacy

Classroom activities to engage students in thinking,
exploring, and making sense of the world

SANDRA MIRABELLI

LIONEL SANDNER

Pembroke Publishers Limited

© 2023 Pembroke Publishers
538 Hood Road
Markham, Ontario, Canada L3R 3K9
www.pembrokepublishers.com

Library and Archives Canada Cataloguing in Publication

Title: Fail-safe strategies for science & literacy : classroom activities to engage students in thinking, exploring, and making sense of the world / Sandra Mirabelli & Lionel Sandner.

Other titles: Fail-safe strategies for science and literacy

Names: Mirabelli, Sandra, author. | Sandner, Lionel, author.

Description: Includes bibliographical references and index.

Identifiers: Canadiana (print) 20230483267 | Canadiana (ebook) 20230483291 | ISBN 9781551383644 (softcover) | ISBN 9781551389639 (PDF)

Subjects: LCSH: Science—Study and teaching (Elementary)

Classification: LCC LB1585 .M57 2023 | DDC 372.35—dc23

Editor: Kat Mototsune
Cover Design: John Zehethofer
Typesetting: Jay Tee Graphics Ltd.

Printed and bound in Canada
9 8 7 6 5 4 3 2 1

Contents

Preface

It would have been hard to believe, when a literacy consultant (Sandra) joined a science implementation team (including Lionel) in 2010, that a book on integrating these two subjects would emerge. And yet that's exactly what happened. Working together, we both realized we had more in common than differences. That "aha!" moment led us to build a science-literacy professional learning community with teachers in one of Canada's largest school boards. And we sustained our program for seven years. Working with the same teachers each year allowed us to explore new ideas on how to integrate literacy into science and vice versa. Eventually, our participants told us we should write a book, because our days with them were the best professional development they had ever had. We wish we could say we began writing immediately, but taking our classroom ideas to print took a pandemic! And here we are. We're happy to have you join us on this journey.

Our vision for this book is that it will help teachers feel comfortable and confident teaching science through a literacy-integrated approach. This vision and our confidence that it is possible came out of our seven-year collaboration in Sandra's school board. Year after year, more and more folks would join our exploration of the connections between science and literacy. And year after year, we kept finding more ways to connect the two subjects, sprinkling in some math, information technology, and art along the way. It was the ultimate professional development for our educators and for us.

Working with the same educators for seven years allowed us to explore ideas and get immediate teacher feedback on the viability of those ideas in the classroom. We kept and developed the ideas that worked, tossed out the others, and moved on. In the world of design and technology, they call this prototyping. In education, we call it learning! And the more learning we did, the more we connected our ideas to other subject areas.

Connecting people and ideas became our superpower. Using this superpower when working with teachers made us realize the importance of pedagogy first. Making science about doing and thinking was motivating for everyone.

Embedding literacy strategies and skills offered all learners a new entry point into understanding science. And these same strategies provided formative assessment data for planning next steps. We came to understand that, if we engage students' curiosity and sense of wonder, students' persistence and stamina with tasks and in problem-solving come along too. In the process, teachers rediscovered that learning can be fun!

While the debate over whether an integrated approach with science at the core should be STEM- or STEAM-focused heated up in education, we were finding that the one letter that was making a real difference for us, our educators, and their students was not *A*, but was instead *L* for Literacy! We like to call it STEM-L.

We acknowledge that the current environment in education does not necessarily start with a focus on subject areas. But we also believe that you, the reader, got into education because you were passionate about helping others and have a love for one or more subjects found in all our schools. At the same time, the classroom environment is foundational to productive learning, so let's agree that built into the DNA of every school are the following facts:

- Relationships are the most important aspect of any school.
- Schools are respectful, safe places for all to learn.
- Students need to be supported to reach their potential because they learn at different rates.
- When both students and teachers see themselves as learners, great things can happen!

Introduction

Now that you've got this far in the book, we have a confession to make. We don't believe that fail-safe strategies are those designed to always work perfectly. What we really like about the term *fail-safe* is that it implies you can use a strategy, not without failing, but without fear of failure. In learning, as in life, it takes hard work and failure to be successful. Stanislas Dehaene states in *How We Learn*, "It is practically impossible to progress if we didn't start off by failing" (Dehaene, 2018). We believe you'll forgive us for playing with semantics if we can show you how combining literacy and science into your practice in the classroom will make you a better teacher and, by extension, help your students grow.

Somewhere during the development of this book, we came across a definition for FAIL as *First Attempt In Learning*. It resonated for us.

As educators, first attempts can be the most challenging part of changing and improving our practices. When we started working together, we had to take that first step as we ventured into each other's educational domains. And trust us, we tripped up many times as we learned from our mistakes and failures. Now Lionel knows about phonemic awareness and Sandra is a pro at science demonstrations involving Newton's Laws. It is our belief you can bring your strengths to this book and use our ideas in either science or literacy to become a better teacher. Let's change the definition of *fail-safe* from "guaranteed to not fail" to "creating a classroom environment where it is safe to fail so that we may learn together in a safe space for all."

In this book we address what our teachers perceived as the most challenging aspect of teaching science at the elementary-school level—the "doing" of science. Our approach positions literacy strategies as a fail-safe mechanism and multi-modal approach to science learning. These fail-safe strategies will have students talking, listening, writing, visualizing, and reading/viewing as they participate in the "doing" of hands-on, minds-on science activities. Ultimately, the strategies work as sensemaking tools to build content knowledge in science. Pairing the science activities in this book with literacy strategies also helps us work toward a broader goal of developing five thinking routines that we believe will serve students well in all areas of their learning and will help them think about and make sense of the world around them.

This book is for you if you are looking to

- bring fun, hands-on learning into your classroom
- expand your literacy strategy toolkit to support learning in science
- help students develop five thinking routines essential for processing across subject areas
- build your content knowledge of science
- develop your know-how in teaching science and language arts
- gather formative assessment data with ease
- become aware of research that supports an integrated science-and-literacy approach and its benefits for teaching and learning

This book is for

- new teachers looking to improve their practice and expand their repertoire of literacy strategies and science activities
- experienced teachers looking to add new and fun activities and strategies to their existing repertoire to promote student thinking and understanding
- professional development leaders and school-board consultants providing professional learning for in-service teachers in their districts
- department heads and subject leads looking to start a book club
- pre-service teachers looking for practical activities and strategies they can implement in their teaching blocks
- faculty of education professors and instructors looking for a supplementary text that provides practical activities and strategies supported by evidence and theory

In short, if you are looking to implement good ideas that work in the classroom, this book is for you!

How to Use This Book

There are several ways you can navigate through this book. Here are a few suggestions:

- Start at the beginning and make your way through each chapter. With this approach, you will be introduced to new ideas and discover an effective approach to teaching and learning that has science and language arts working together.
- If you are interested in some of the cognitive science that supports our approach and informs our thinking, check out the first part of Chapter 2: From Cognitive Science to Thinking Routines. We will introduce you to current research and knowledge that helps us make sense of how learning happens.
- Start with Chapter 1: Science and Literacy Together if you're curious about how we combined the two disciplines. This section will give you the background information you need to understand where science and literacy intersect.
- Start with the second part of Chapter 2: From Cognitive Science to Thinking Routines if you are curious about how the research has inspired new ideas. It introduces the five thinking routines we teach students to use to

process information and promote an understanding of phenomena, concepts, problems, and issues in science.

- If literacy is your strength, you could start with the chart at the beginning of Part 2 (pages 51–53) and take a look at the Literacy Strategy column. Start with strategies you recognize and see what they look like when coupled with science content. Then try unfamiliar strategies in any context to get a feel for them in your classroom. When you are comfortable with a strategy, check out the science activity we have used with it and try it out with your students in science class.

- If science is your strength, you could start with the chart at the beginning of Part 2 (pages 51–53) and take a look at the Science Activity column. Reacquaint yourself with the activities and check out our tips and videos for effective ways to introduce or use these activities. Also make sure to check out the Fail-Safe Strategy that we have paired with each activity. These literacy strategies offer support as you work through science activities with your class. Be sure to go back and try out some activities you haven't done or heard of before.

- If you need an activity for tomorrow, scan the list of science activities in the chart at the beginning of Part 2 (pages 51–53). Choose one that highlights a skill you would like to focus on at this point in the year. Or choose one that will engage your class and stimulate the kind of thinking you would like to promote in your classroom.

These same suggestions would work in a book club or professional development network. The key is to start where there is interest and build from there!

We would love to hear and see what you're doing. You can always share how it's going by finding us at failsafestrategies.com.

PART **1**

Thinking Routines Linking Science and Literacy

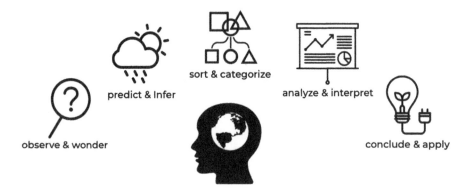

observe & wonder

predict & Infer

sort & categorize

analyze & interpret

conclude & apply

Thinking Routines

CHAPTER 1

Science and Literacy Together

Our work with science educators was the result of a larger movement in science education to bring about a change in classroom practice from *reading* about science to *doing* science. Coupled with this was a parallel movement in literacy to incorporate a content literacy approach and later a disciplinary literacy approach to support students in making sense of subject-specific content. For us, this became an important opportunity to support educators in finding authentic intersections between science and literacy in their classrooms. The integration of a topic-based curriculum (science) with a skills-based curriculum (language arts and literacy) made sense to us. As it has often been said, "If we want students to think, we need to give them something worth thinking about." Science and literacy together were just what we needed. It seems intuitive that it just works.

As we began to look, we discovered there was plenty of existing research supporting the integration of science and literacy. Pearson, Moje, and Greenleaf (2010) note, "Literacy is best enacted as a set of learning tools that support knowledge acquisition rather than as a set of independent curriculum goals." The more time we spent looking, the more we realized our thinking was well supported by research. Our sense that it just works was much like Gladwell's (2005) premise in *Blink*—what seemed like intuition was really based on a wealth of background knowledge and experience that we had accumulated over the years and were now applying in novel ways.

Let's take a closer look at why science and literacy work together, based on our observations, experiences, and supporting research.

- Integration creates many efficiencies in a vast curriculum where time to teach science has decreased over the years, as more time has been allocated to language arts and math (Drake, Reid & Kolohon, 2014; Fries-Gaither & Shiverdecker, 2013). By using science content as the context for reading, writing, and talking in language arts, we increase the amount of time devoted to science teaching and learning. Reading to build background knowledge or to explore science phenomena, and working with scientific vocabulary and writing as a means to process thinking or report findings became part of language-arts time. Time devoted to science could now be spent investigating, inquiring, and doing science.

- An integrated approach reduces duplication (Drake et al., 2014). As we bundled related expectations across both curricula, we reduced the demands on students to complete numerous performance tasks in order to provide us with evidence of learning. A focus in language arts on different text forms offered a variety of ways for students to represent their growing understanding of science. Students could examine the format of an infographic in media studies, then apply this literacy knowledge and format to communicate what they were learning about science topics like GMOs, or to explore STEM issues like increasing world food production.

- Integrating science and literacy sparks curiosity and aligns more closely with how we experience the world. Students are curious about the world around them and wonder how things work. They have all sorts of questions that cut across subject boundaries. While separating disciplines into unique time compartments and curricula has been efficient for schooling, students' observations and wonderings remind us that we experience the world in a more holistic and integrated way. An integrated approach helps students connect instruction to their interests and current understandings (Hattie, 2009) and, in the process, makes the curriculum relevant to them. An integrated understanding of concepts and ideas also helps students build a richly connected web of knowledge or schema that they can access later for problem-solving and decision-making (Krajcik, 2014; Fisher, Frey & Hattie, 2016; Willingham, D.T., 2006).

- Language-arts class provides valuable time to build students' background knowledge about the natural world. From a literacy perspective, research shows that the background knowledge a student brings to a text and learning is the strongest predictor of reading comprehension (Neuman, Kaefer & Pinkman, 2014; Cervetti & Hiebert, 2018; Fisher & Frey, 2009; Willingham, 2017, 2021; Wexler, 2020). As Willingham (2021) reminds us, "Knowing things makes it easier to learn new things" (p. 38). In science and STEM, scientific background knowledge helps students make predictions about what might happen in an investigation. It also allows them to draw inferences from collected data and to connect and extend their understanding of phenomena, concepts, and topics. For us, language arts became the right time to introduce engaging supplementary science texts on grade-level phenomena, concepts, and topics, and to build scientific knowledge when there wasn't much background knowledge to activate. By doing this, we could help all students develop an organized and usable schema from which they could retrieve relevant background knowledge in science class (Fisher & Frey, 2009; Neuman, S.B., 2019; Willingham, D. T., 2006).

- Science concepts and texts can be complex. Technical vocabulary, theoretical and abstract ideas, and the variety and complexity of informational text structures make for challenging learning (Fries-Gaither & Shiverdecker, 2013; Fang, Lamme & Pringle, 2010). During language-arts time, it is important to ensure that we are supporting students with the skills and strategies they need to read nonfiction texts; for example, explicitly teaching how to detect the text structures writers use to write about a science concept and the morphology of science vocabulary. We need to support students in unlocking these complexities to help them make sense of what they are learning.

- Science and literacy are both concerned with studying and communicating our understanding of the world. In this way, the two disciplines have similar goals. The content of science provides students with compelling reasons to read, write, and talk in the language-arts classroom (Fang, Lamme, Pringle, 2010; Fries-Gaither & Shiverdecker, 2013). By engaging in science and literacy together, we not only prompt students to use their literacy skills and scientific thinking to document investigations, observations, and the data they are collecting, but also to discuss, debate, question, ponder, and explore science phenomena with classmates to gain more insight into the world around them (Cervetti, Pearson, Barber et al, 2007; Pearson, Moje, Greenleaf, 2010).

- There are many natural overlaps of cognitive skills and thinking processes used in science with those used in language arts. Predicting, inferring, questioning, classifying and organizing data, making connections between what students are seeing or reading and their own lives, collecting evidence and making judgments—these are just a few of the common skills shared by scientists, readers, and writers (Pearson et al., 2010; Fang et al., 2010; Fries-Gaither & Shiverdecker, 2013; Cervetti, Pearson, Barber et al., 2007). They are also skills important to supporting inquiry-based learning in many subjects. Pairing literacy strategies with science activities that develop these skills in both disciplines allows us to support students in original and novel ways.

- We discovered another overlap—scientific thinking and habits of mind are related to critical thinking and critical media literacy. Whether we were in science class or language arts, strategies for building a healthy skepticism about media reports on science-related topics benefitted from skill development in both disciplines. Both science and literacy can teach us about posing the right questions, about verifying the authenticity of information and sources, about examining the evidence used to support claims, and about the importance of consulting multiple sources. By learning how to read the news like a scientist, students develop critical media literacy that can help them detect possible misinformation in their everyday lives (Howell & Brossard, 2020; Aviv & Baram-Tsabari, 2020).

It wasn't long before our network teachers reported students were more engaged in both science and language arts because of our integrated approach. The topics and issues of science were compelling. One of our teachers reported that one day students started spontaneously debating whether it was more appropriate and beneficial to fund space exploration or underwater exploration. Another teacher shared that Grade 9 science averages at midterm for students who had experienced an integrated approach in Grades 7 and 8 were "consistently in the 70% range or higher, and no one was failing science!" In fact, empirical research on integration in general, and on science and literacy taught together specifically, has provided evidence of significant improvements in student engagement and learning (Fang & Wei, 2010; Cervetti, Pearson, Bravo, Barber, 2006; Drake et al., 2014; Yore, Bisanz & Hand, 2003).

CHAPTER 2

From Cognitive Science to Thinking Routines

A teacher's constant challenge is to find engaging ideas to bring into the classroom. There are two steps in bringing an idea to fruition and they are both surprisingly difficult. First, you must find the idea. In theory, finding the idea should be easy. Go online, search the concept you're about to teach, and pick the best one. The problem comes with finding the best one. There is no shortage of ideas, but which one will work? That's where we hope you trust that we know what works. Secondly, you have to operationalize the idea. What is the best way to plan and bring your idea to life? There are so many competing interests in this step, it becomes a challenge. How do you engage students? What concept are you covering? How can you connect to the curriculum, plan for differentiation, and assess student progress? It is easy to become overwhelmed by all the challenges and, in the end, just stick to notes and worksheets. And sometimes that's totally fine. But having a coherent plan that allows for integration between subjects, success for all students with different abilities, and deep learning is the ultimate goal. And that's where combining best-practice research on cognition with many years of teaching experience gives you the fail-safe strategies to integrate science into your literacy classes.

Cognitive Science: How the Brain Learns

What follows is not an exhaustive explanation of how the brain learns, but rather a journey through some key ideas that we feel can help guide your practice. They form the foundation of our fail-safe strategies.

Before exploring fail-safe strategies, let's focus on a foundational question related to our practice. How do students learn? There are many theories around the way the brain learns. At the core of these theories is understanding how an idea or experience moves through our brain, from paying attention to words or sounds, through passing that information to our working memory, and finally integrating this information into our long-term memory. This process has been a fascination of ours, since knowing how our students learn guides our practice.

We've all encountered situations in which a class progresses as expected, and then suddenly learning difficulties arise. Early in our careers, we found this frustrating. Students showed progress until the chapter on fractions or the one on word problems. Or everyone could understand the chemistry lesson until balancing equations puzzled a third of the class. As our teaching experience deepened, we found strategies to address some of these issues. However, there remained a nagging question in our minds as to why these difficulties arise. Based on our observations, it appeared that something was happening in the students' brains that prevented them from processing this newly acquired information. To solve the problem, we needed to look at cognitive science research on how the brain learns.

There are a variety of theories describing how the brain learns, but the models we align with are the Information Processing Model (IPM) and, related to IPM, Cognitive Load Multimedia Learning (CLMT) Theory.

We will focus on the three memory systems in order: Sensory, Working, and Long-term.

First proposed by Atkinson and Shiffrin (1968) and expanded upon by Baddeley and Hitch (1974, 1999), the IPM explains how the brain takes in information from the surroundings and processes that information. You might recall some or all of these terms from your university psychology classes, but the last twenty years of research have extended our understanding of how we take in words and sounds through our eyes and ears, and process that information through our working memory. This new information is then integrated into what we already know, the background information stored in our long-term memory. Using this diagram based on Chew (2021), it is possible to track the key steps in taking information from the learning environment to long-term memory.

Information Processing Model (IPM) adapted from Chew (2021)

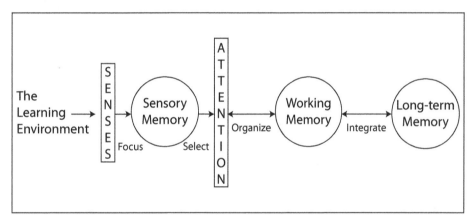

Sensory Memory

Sensory memory refers to how each of us decides what visual and auditory signals we will pay attention to and pass on to our working memory. A signal could be audio (a voice) or visual (an image). In that moment of receiving the signal, there is unlimited capacity to choose what is important to us; based on our choice, the information in that signal is passed to our working memory.

Note that the IPM does not separate audio and visual signals. That will come into our discussion later.

In the IPM diagram above, you can observe that attention plays a big part in learning materials entering the working memory. In the classroom, at home, and in the world outside these two areas, there are many stimuli competing for our attention. As humans, we select and focus on a stimulus for a variety of reasons. Maybe it's interesting, maybe it's dangerous, or maybe it's novel and we're curious about it. As most teachers know, this range of stimuli can make it difficult for our students to select and focus on a lesson or activity. We're sure your school has had to deal with the proliferation of mobile devices in our students' hands. The IPM model clearly points out that, if you're focused on your screen for non-learning reasons, the wrong information is getting into your brain. Our intent is to provide you with strategies to help your students focus on the activity in your class and not the latest viral trend on social media.

Working Memory

After we pay attention and select the information, it is passed to the working memory. Here is where the information is organized. Unfortunately, this is not a simple process. And this is where our problems around learning fractions, solving word problems, or balancing chemical equations begin.

Educators can focus on the fact that, for information to be learned or skills to be acquired in long-term memory, everything must be processed through short-term, or working, memory. The working memory is the gatekeeper to anything reaching our long-term memory. Long-term memory is amazing because it can hold limitless amounts of experience and information, but working memory can hold only between four and nine chunks of any kind of information at any one time. Current research suggests that the working memory can hold no more than four chunks or pieces of new, relevant information. So it is incumbent on educators to ensure any lesson or activity does not overload the working memory.

Cognitive Load Theory

How do we create lessons that prevent an overload? Cognitive Load Theory provides research on why using fail-safe strategies in your classroom can begin to address working memory limits. Rooted in work by John Sweller, Cognitive Load Theory (CLT) starts from the idea that working memory is limited. Every time we learn something, we need to consider the cognitive load required to take in the knowledge, skill(s), and/or ability(ies) (KSA). Put another way, a cognitive load requires the brain to allocate working memory to any given task. The exciting part of CLT is the discovery that cognitive loads can be managed by purposeful design of instructional materials. Let's examine how cognitive load is handled in the working memory.

There are three types of cognitive load processed through the working memory: intrinsic, extraneous, and germane. Each load has a specific role in the working memory, but the most important thing to remember is that the overall cognitive load of these three types cannot exceed the capacity of the working memory. If it does, the information is too complex and the learner will be unsuccessful in learning the concept. Put as an equation:

$$\text{Intrinsic Load} + \text{Extraneous Load} + \text{Germane Load} + \text{Free Working Memory} = \text{Working Memory Capacity}$$

- Intrinsic load is related to the inherent difficulty of the material. It cannot be manipulated by purposeful design. The difficulty of the material is described by the element interactivity of the knowledge to be learned, with an element being anything that needs to be learned or has been learned, such as a concept or a procedure (Sweller, 2010). So, for example, learning your times tables takes a learning task that initially has high element interactivity and reduces it to low interactivity. For a novice learner, learning $3 \times 8 = 24$ is considered high element interactivity: the student would have to hold the numbers 3 and 8 in their working memory, along with the concept of multiplication, to figure out the answer is 24. Once this fact is in long-term memory, however, it can be recalled with minimal effort and no impact on the working memory, and here the concept has low element interactivity. Knowing the times tables creates space in the working memory to learn concepts with a higher element interactivity, like fractions or physics problems. When planning any unit, lesson, or activity, the goal is to ensure the intrinsic load is maintained and not added to.

- Extraneous load relates to the cognitive effort required to find the information. The goal in planning is to remove any material that is not relevant to the learning process. For example, extra images or animations not related to the material to be learned in a slide deck can be considered extraneous.
- Germane load represents the cognitive effort required to internalize the KSA into long-term memory. Again, germane load can be fostered by purposeful design. In learning any KSA, time must be spent reflecting and processing the information in a meaningful manner so that it can be placed into long-term memory. Metacognitive activities or strategies are part of the germane cognitive load.

Long-Term Memory

Combined with the cognitive loads operating within the working memory are the prior experiences and metacognitive skills that every learner has in their long-term memory. The brain's long-term memory can hold an unlimited amount of experiences. Looking at the IPM model on page 15, we see that long-term memory stores the signals taken in by the sensory system and processed by the working memory. Once the information is deeply encoded into the long-term memory, it can be retrieved at any time to help a person solve a current problem.

Brown (2014) defines learning as "acquiring knowledge and skills and having them readily available from memory so you can make sense of figure problems and opportunities." Coming across this definition was an "aha!" moment for us. Learning isn't the result of pouring information into a student, as the old metaphor suggests. In addition, it is not simply about being exposed to a concept, although that can be helpful. In order to learn, one must apply what one already knows. But how do you acquire knowledge and integrate it into your long-term memory?

Efrat Furst (2018) created a model that shows how knowledge is represented in long-term memory over time. There are four conceptual stages—*knowing, understanding, using,* and *mastery*—that reflect what we do with information in our long-term memory.

Diagrams of the stages below created by Mohsin Nabeel.

During this stage, reducing distractions, focusing attention, and introducing concepts separately should be the focus of the educator.

Knowing	
When we learn something new, the concept is isolated in the long-term memory. It has been recognized to fit within some area of our prior knowledge, but is not connected to any of our prior knowledge. For example, we are introduced to a new piece of science equipment.	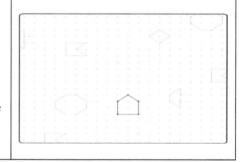

During this stage, learners need explanations, models, analogies, and a range of different contexts to help them build their understanding.

Understanding

The new piece of information is connected to other knowledge we have, so that meaning is created. In the diagram, we see one of the concept nodes being connected to some knowledge already in long-term memory. For example, we use the new piece of science equipment in a lab and begin to understand its purpose.

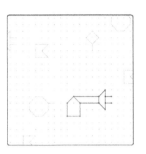

During this stage, the learner is answering questions and using cognitive science-based techniques like retrieval practice.

Using

In this stage, the concept becomes functional. The diagram shows more connections to the concept from our prior knowledge being made as the concept is used in different contexts. For example, the science equipment is used in different types of activities.

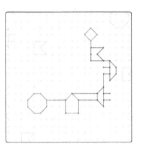

During this stage, we draw on current research in cognitive science to provide spaced and interleaved practice, so the learner strengthens the connections between prior knowledge and the concept.

Mastery

In stage four, the concept is used many times in different contexts until a state of mastery is achieved. With each practice, the pathways become more robust and efficient. The diagram shows pathways being dropped (increased efficiency) and becoming darker (more robust). For example, the learner can carry out their own activity and select the piece of equipment required to solve a problem.

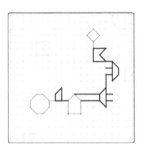

Now we can start to build some insight into why those fraction, word problems, and chemical balancing concepts are difficult for our students. If they don't have the background knowledge, then there is nothing for them to integrate the information in their working memory with. Their working memory quickly becomes overloaded and the information flow stops. We've all had to stop the lesson and back up to cover information that has clearly been forgotten or misunderstood. In effect, we're going back to a spot where students' background knowledge can be used to integrate the information in the working memory. In this process, you're strengthening the linkages between concepts, so new information can be added to the framework. Brown's definition of learning can be extended to show that retrieving information from long-term memory involves strengthening the existing connections; to paraphrase Hebb's (1949) famous statement, "Connections that are used together, stay together." And each time we retrieve that information, our long-term memory gets strengthened and our understanding gets stronger.

Another point from Furst's model is the importance of the Using and Mastery stages. In a busy school day, it's easy to forget that students need continual practice in using key concepts. It's not that they don't try; it's that they simply forget.

Forgetting curve based on the work of Hermann Ebbinghaus (1885)

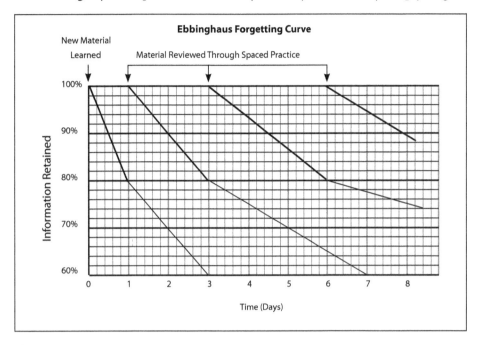

The Ebbinghaus Forgetting Curve shows that, as soon as we're presented with information, we begin to forget. By the second day without review, we've forgotten 30% of what we learned. Luckily, there's a solution to this natural forgetting. We just need a reminder. That reminder tops up our memory. Using Furst's model, review strengthens the connections in our long-term memory because we're using the information. And this also explains why Brown's definition of learning is so powerful. Learning is the use of information we have retrieved from our long-term memory. We're strengthening those connections we have already created. So whether it's fractions, word problems, or chemical equations, if we have no experience or have missed a key step in the learning process to get to these concepts, we're going to experience difficulty when introduced to the new concepts.

Schema and Automation

Furst's model (pages 17–18) shows that knowledge and skills in our long-term memory are organized into schema. A schema is an organized framework of long-term knowledge that, when activated, facilitates the encoding and learning of new, related concepts; promotes inference, reasoning, and problem-solving within that domain; and guides recall of relevant information (Chen, 2021). And the better we have mastered, or made connections in our long-term memory, the more automatic the recall and use of the knowledge and skills. If the knowledge and skills cannot be retrieved with reliable automaticity, then more time must be spent understanding and mastering them.

There is clear evidence for the importance of learning knowledge and skills that are foundational to learning new concepts. While the most obvious examples are for strong literacy and numeracy skills, mastering times tables for math, periodic table names and symbols for chemistry, and decoding skills for language arts to the point of automaticity opens the doors for further learning. Imagine trying to solve a math problem or infer the author's meaning in a short story if you could not automatically access schema related to times tables or word recognition. The IPM highlights the importance of being able to automatically retrieve and use key knowledge and skills.

Active Processing and Learning

Current research has extended the IPM to the Cognitive Load Multimedia Theory (CLMT), which accounts for the fact that we can take in information through the sensory memory with both audio and visual signals.

Adapted from Mayer and Moreno (2003)

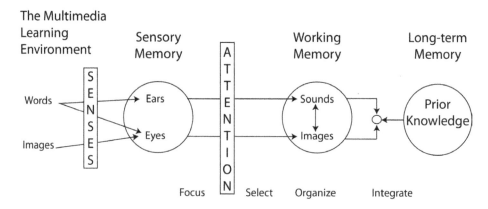

There are three important concepts related to the process of learning in CLMT compared to IPM:

1. In the sensory memory, the eyes are used for selecting images and the ears for selecting words.
2. Once the student has paid attention to the information, the words and images are passed to the working memory. Here the sounds and words are organized.
3. CLMT expands on the IPM model by showing how long-term memory can take the information organized in the working memory and integrate it with prior knowledge.

CLMT expands on the IPM's use of the terms *select*, *organize*, and *integrate*. Failsafe strategies are designed to support students to *select* the correct information and *organize* it in a manner that supports them in *integrating* their new understanding into their long-term memory.

Using the CLMT model, Mayer (2022, p. 59) describes three assumptions that underlie how people learn:

Multimedia learning refers to the fact people learn better from words and images than from words alone. Mayer (2022) states, "CLMT describes how people learn from words and pictures based on empirical research evidence and on consensus theoretical principles in cognitive science."

1. Dual Channels: Humans possess separate channels for processing visual and auditory information. This builds on work by Baddeley (1999) and Paivio (1986).
2. Limited Capacity: Humans are limited in the amount of information that can be processed in each channel at one time. This builds on work by Baddeley (1999), Sweller, Ayers and Kalyuga (2011).
3. Active Process: Humans engage in active learning by attending to relevant incoming information, organizing selected information into coherent mental representations, and integrating mental representations with other knowledge. This builds on work by Mayer (2021) and Wittrock (1989).

These assumptions form the backbone of our program. Everything we do with students acknowledges the importance of dual channels for taking in information, of limited working memory, and of actively processing information to learn.

CLMT forms the foundation for active or meaningful learning to occur in the STEM–L classroom. For any activity we use, our goal is to ensure that

- the material is clear, concise, and coherent
- guidance is provided to the student for connecting the activity to their current background knowledge

What does this look like in the classroom? Based on our experience, we believe there is a framework of five thinking routines that will allow you to use the ideas from cognitive science in your practice.

The Five Thinking Routines

"Children must be taught how to think, not what to think."
— Margaret Mead (1928)

As we reflected on what we know now about how students learn, on our own classroom experiences, and on working over seven years with elementary teachers bringing science and literacy together, our driving question became *How can we help students build schema so that they can make sense of complex science concepts, phenomena, problems, and issues?*

In our work with our science literacy network teachers, all sorts of related questions had come up. How do we prepare our students to think critically to ensure they can distinguish misinformation encountered on social media from scientific evidence and facts? How do we encourage our students to think creatively to solve today's problems and issues, and old ones that have persisted for decades? How do we teach our students to think analytically to make sense of all the statistics and scientific data that they encounter on a daily basis? How do we teach them to be flexible and adaptable in their thinking when they are faced with unexpected challenges that require them to think outside the box? For us, all these questions revealed that students need a dependable toolkit of thinking skills—a toolkit that will help them make sense of and continually adapt to a world where change is the only constant. The more we reflected on this, the more we realized that our thinking toolkit should eventually be so ingrained in how students work that it would become a routine part of how they operate. In other words, we needed to develop routines that would "become part of the fabric of the classroom through repeated use" (Ritchhart, R., Church, M., Morrison, K., 2011, p. 48).

The concept of thinking routines is not new. But how we envision them is. And that matters. If you have read about the importance of establishing thinking routines in your classroom before, it was likely at a strategy level. The challenge for us was considering how students could automate so many strategies, each with its own set of steps. As we considered the cognitive science about how the brain learns, we recognized that, for us, thinking routines were really about a small set of key skills we want students to automate so they become part of a student's procedural knowledge. By automating skills students need to use frequently, we can help students work around the limits of their working memories (Hartman, J., Nelson, E. & Kirschner, P., 2022, p. 249). This was the key: automating important skills would make our students better problem-solvers who could be flexible, critical, creative, and analytical thinkers!

We realized that it is the automaticity of certain skills that differentiates an expert from a novice in problem-solving situations. Research comparing experts with novices emphasizes the importance of automaticity. As Kirschner and Hendrick (2020) point out, students are

> …novices, not little experts…When encountering a new problem, experts think in a very solution-oriented way and their prior knowledge is mainly procedural in nature about how to tackle a problem along with a deep conceptual knowledge about the conditions under which the procedures can be applied.

Automaticity of some knowledge and procedures would free up space in students' working memory so they could attend to more complex aspects of a problem.

It became evident that what we wanted to develop would be the result of our combined STEM and literacy knowledge and expertise. The goal was to establish a set of thinking routines that would become automatic over time, allowing students to focus on other parts of complex problems. Our challenge was to create a system that would enable students to assess and evaluate content they encounter through reading and viewing. This would not only assist students with decision-making and problem-solving processes, but also empower them to develop deeper understandings of novel situations while activating the healthy skepticism they need to make sense of the world we live in today.

We knew that many skills—observing, questioning, predicting, inferring, organizing and classifying data, making connections, analyzing, interpreting, and drawing conclusions—were commonly used in both science and language arts. We wondered—could our thinking routines come from the intersection of these science processing skills and important thinking skills in language arts and literacy?

In our work with science educators, we had already been pairing some thinking skills together quite naturally. For example, when we focused on making good observations in science class, this seamlessly led to supporting students in generating questions as a next step. *Observing* initiated a first engagement for students with the experience or phenomenon we were studying. *Wondering* as a second step enabled students to process the experience for deeper insight and connection to their prior knowledge. Educators shared that their students seamlessly engaged in this two-step process, since it was a natural progression in their thinking. Based on these experiences and our understanding that students need to work within the capacity of their working memory, we continued to pair common skills from science and literacy in this way.

The result is a set of five thinking routines designed to help students break down the complexity of a phenomenon or problem into manageable chunks that are within their working memory capacity:

1. Observe and Wonder
2. Predict and Infer
3. Sort and Categorize
4. Analyze and Interpret
5. Conclude and Apply

As a system of paired skills, the thinking routines are designed to reduce the cognitive load associated with learning. The first skill in each pair provides initial engagement with an experience, phenomenon, or data, while the second skill is used to initiate further processing for understanding and connection to schema.

The use of paired skills is based on Cognitive Load Theory and the idea of automaticity, where tasks become easier with practice and require less conscious effort.

These routines or skill sets will help students think deeply about content, identify patterns and relationships, and draw meaningful conclusions.

Thinking Routine	Students will...
Observe and Wonder	• Use their senses to gather information about the characteristics and changes in an object or event in order to spark their curiosity • Ask questions to connect to prior knowledge and get a better understanding of what they're learning
Predict and Infer	• Predict what will happen, based on their prior experience, knowledge, and current observations • Infer a logical conclusion about a situation or event based on their scientific background knowledge and reasoning skills
Sort and Categorize	• Create order out of data or objects that at first seem random or unordered, based on similarities • Identify why items are grouped together, based on attributes or relationships they see
Analyze and Interpret	• Look at data collected in an investigation to see how all the parts fit together • Reassemble the parts to tell a complete story and better understand the data
Conclude and Apply	• Explain what they have learned about the phenomenon being studied and why it matters • Use their knowledge and skills in a new context or situation because it is appropriate, relevant, and useful

To support students in developing these important thinking routines we have also developed a set of tools, or fail-safe strategies, that provide students with the necessary guidance to apply the thinking routines to a range of different situations and problems. The strategies are fail-safe in that they provide a structure to help students practice their thinking skills in a safe, low-stakes environment, so they can develop the confidence to use their thinking skills in any situation. Together, the thinking routines and the fail-safe strategies provide an explicit and systematic way for students to build schema and make sense of science concepts and phenomena.

A Closer Look at the Thinking Routines

The charts that follow will support you in building a common language with students about each of the skills in a pairing. The charts define each skill and identify why it is important; notes in the margin refer to research that supports the use of these skills in the classroom. We think you will also see that these five thinking routines are easily transferable to all disciplines. They help students make connections, engage in critical thinking, and better understand the world around them.

Connecting to Research

The brain is a natural pattern-seeker, analyzer, and interpreter. It strives to figure out things and is rewarded chemically when it does. Slowing down the looking is important to prevent the brain from filling in gaps and possibly jumping to inaccurate conclusions. Together, the skills of observing and wondering help activate the brain so that it is alert and ready to learn as it searches for answers, enjoys what it is learning, and, in the process, becomes more persistent and better able to remember what it has learned. (Zadina, J., 2014; Stenger, M., 2014)

Thinking Routine: Observe and Wonder

Observe

What is it?

Observing is looking closely to describe an object, situation, or event. Making good observations requires engaging all five senses to gather information related to the physical properties and characteristics of, and changes occurring to, an object or during an event.

Why is it important?

Slowing down the looking is key to helping students see details and detect patterns. It prompts students to consider finer details they might overlook at first. Careful observation will help students more successfully engage in the other thinking routines; e.g., sort and classify, predict and infer.

Fail-Safe Strategies to try:
- See, Think, Wonder (page 54)
- Wait… What? (page 58)
- Before and After Diagrams (page 63)

Wonder

What is it?

Wonder is sparked by curiosity. It's a type of thinking we do when we are interested in finding out more about something. Wonder motivates us to search for answers. Wondering, or asking questions, is a fundamental skill in science that leads to inquiry and investigation.

Why is it important?

When students wonder or ask questions, they are more active and self-directed in their learning. Wonder sparks conversation and can encourage students to exchange ideas with each other. It also promotes connections to prior knowledge and motivates students to search for a deeper understanding of the phenomenon being studied. Wonder makes learning relevant and meaningful.

Fail-Safe Strategies to try:
- Q-Chart Question Prompts (page 71)
- Think, Question, Explore (page 68)

How are these skills connected?

Good observation skills actively engage students with the phenomenon being examined and often naturally lead them to wonder and ask new questions. The act of wondering or questioning propels the learning or quest forward.

Thinking Routine: Predict and Infer

Predict

What is it?

A prediction is a particular kind of inference that is future-focused. Making predictions has the student anticipate what will happen in a future event, based on prior scientific knowledge, experiences, research, and possibly observations they are currently making. A prediction is not a wild guess. Because it does not ask you to explain why you think something will happen, it is not a hypothesis either.

Infer

What is it?

When we ask students to make an inference, we are asking them to examine evidence and use their scientific background knowledge and reasoning skills to draw a logical conclusion about a situation or event. Inferences go beyond what is observable. Inferences help explain what is happening or how a situation came to be. Inferential thinking can help students generate a hypothesis about a situation or event.

Connecting to Research

Inferential thinking engages students more actively in learning by sparking curiosity and increasing motivation. Students become detectives, as they put the evidence together with their scientific knowledge to find missing information or clear up a mystery. When students make predictions, they become emotionally invested in verifying whether they were correct, increasing their attention. The possible element of surprise, if they are wrong, can facilitate better transfer to and retrieval from long-term memory (Brod, G., 2021). Making better and correct predictions and inferences relies on students having a wealth of background knowledge on a variety of topics. A broad knowledge base to retrieve from ensures the associations we make in our memory will be richer and more automatically available to us when we detect connections (Willingham, D.T., 2006).

Why is it important?

Predictions help to drive inquiry and can become the basis for creating new testable questions in science. They also provide a starting point for thinking about observations. The distinguishing characteristic of a prediction is that it can eventually be verified as the activity continues. Will a prediction be confirmed or refuted? There is a lot to learn from either of these situations.

Fail-Safe Strategies to try:
- Predict, Explain, Observe, Explain (PEOE) (page 85)
- Trending Now (page 80)
- Poll Everyone (page 89)

Why is it important?

Good inferences help in the process of analyzing and interpreting scientific phenomena. Working through the process of making good inferences from a set of observations helps students understand how scientists use evidence and their scientific knowledge and experiences to answer questions or hypothesize about situations or events.

Fail-Safe Strategies to try:
- Inference Ladder (page 74)
- Think, Pair, Share, Draw (page 77)

How are these skills connected?

Predictions and inferences both rely on combining our observations of an activity ("evidence in the text," as we say in literacy) with our scientific knowledge and experience. While predictions are mainly focused on forecasting what will happen in the future based on evidence, inferences are interpretations of observations, based on our experiences and scientific knowledge, that can help explain what is happening now or has just happened.

Connecting to Research

Categorizing helps students process data in a way that encourages them to check and integrate it with what they already know. The brain uses its schema to search for and store new information by looking for common elements with something already stored in long-term memory (Hardiman, M. 2012; Reinert, S., Hubener, M., Bonhoeffer, T. et al., 2021). Sorting and categorizing develop students' reasoning abilities, as they decide where to place individual items that could belong to multiple groups.

Thinking Routine: Sort and Categorize

Sort	Categorize
What is it?	*What is it?*
When we sort, we are trying to make sense of a large group of objects or data. We create order out of something that might at first appear unordered or random. To sort a group of objects or data, we look at creating subsets within the larger group, based on similarities among items. We might also consider how these items as a group are different from another subset in the grouping.	Categorizing takes place after we have placed objects or data in groups based on similarities. It is the process of deciding on a label or category that identifies why items are placed together by considering what the relationship is among the items in the group. Categories can be based on a variety of characteristics or attributes, ranging from physical characteristics (e.g., shape, color) to behaviors (e.g., fizzes, sinks, floats), to any other connections students see amongst the objects or data.
Why is it important?	*Why is it important?*
Sorting is important because it helps students think logically as they look at how things are connected or related.	Categorizing allows students to communicate to others how they have organized and grouped data or objects.

Sorting prompts students to create a rule or criterion for how they are grouping items. We are constantly sorting things in real life (laundry, papers, books, etc.) to keep things organized and make sense of the world. Sorting helps to develop our students' reasoning skills.

Fail-Safe Strategies to try:
- Question Sorter (page 93)
- List–Group–Label (page 101)
- Visual Word Sort (page 104)
- Chain Notes (page 98)
- GO with the Flow (page 108)

It is a way for students to share their thinking and reasoning. Categorizing data also helps students work with information in a variety of ways, as they analyze and interpret it. It can help them see what is there, determine what is missing, and ask more questions.

Fail-Safe Strategies to try:
- Question Sorter (page 93)
- List–Group–Label (page 101)
- Chain Notes (page 98)

How are these skills connected?

Both sorting and categorizing involve students in considering the similarities and differences among items. In this process, students have to focus on identifying the characteristics of an object or idea. Categorizing requires students to succinctly name the groupings they have established.

Connecting to Research

Analyzing and interpreting are important steps in the processing of data. The brain actively works to make sense of details so that, when the learner puts the data back together as a whole, the learner has synthesized it into something new and meaningful. This thinking routine helps students engage in global processing/thinking so they can see the bigger picture, because they have first engaged in local processing to examine the parts (Hardiman, 2012).

Thinking Routine: Analyze and Interpret

Analyze

What is it?

Analyzing a text (e.g., chart, table, graph, map) or data in science is an important critical thinking skill. When we ask students to analyze something, we are asking them to break it down into its parts to see how they all fit together. Do we see any patterns, trends, or relationships? Sometimes students will need to think about representing the data differently (e.g., convert a table to a graph) to detect the pattern or trend.

Why is it important?

Taking time to analyze the data collected from an investigation helps us ensure it is being interpreted correctly, so that we can gain insights from that data. Analyzing also helps us see if we are missing anything or need more data to establish a pattern or trend.

Interpret

What is it?

When we ask students to interpret data, we are asking them to put the parts back together into a whole and logically explain what the trends, patterns, or relationships might mean, using scientific knowledge. Interpreting requires students to infer and hypothesize, so that they can reassemble the data in a way that tells a complete story and helps them understand them better.

Why is it important?

By interpreting the data collected in an investigation, students are helping themselves and others make sense of it. This phase in the process of working with data engages their critical and analytical thinking to determine what evidence they have to support their thinking.

Fail-Safe Strategies to try:	Fail-Safe Strategies to try:
• What Makes You Say That? (page 115) • Take Note (page 123) • Connect 2 (page 119) • 3-D GO (page 126) • Frayer Model (page 132)	• What Makes You Say That? (page 115) • Take Note (page 123) • Connect 2 (page 119)

How are these skills connected?

While analyzing has us separate things into their parts, interpreting has us synthesize and put things back together into a new whole. As we analyze, we are looking for patterns. While interpreting, we are explaining those patterns and what they might mean.

Connecting to Research

When students see the relevance of what ,they are learning to their own lives there is a greater likelihood that they will retain that knowledge and transfer it to new learning situations. The ultimate goal of learning, from an educational stance, is transfer, or applying knowledge, skills, and strategies to new situations. For this to happen, students need to be able to detect similarities and differences between past situations and a new context (Fisher, D., Frey, N. & Hattie, J., 2016).

Thinking Routine: Conclude and Apply

Conclude	Apply
What is it? When you draw conclusions in science, you are communicating what you have learned about the phenomenon being studied. Your conclusion is a summary of the results of an activity and could answer a question posed at the start of an investigation, offer a possible explanation for what you saw happening, or make a final claim about the phenomenon under investigation, based on your evidence.	*What is it?* When we apply our knowledge and skills, we are putting what we know to use because we recognize that it would be relevant, appropriate, and useful to a new context or situation we are examining. Applying means we have noticed there are connections we can make from our existing knowledge and skill base to other contexts.
Why is it important? In science, a conclusion is an opportunity to state what you have learned and why this knowledge is important. It's an opportunity to take a step back and look at the bigger picture and context of an investigation and how that affected your results. It provides closure after having examined your evidence.	*Why is it important?* This stage helps students see the relevance and importance of what they are learning. By applying their learning to a new context (familiar or different) students take responsibility for their learning. They are determining that it would be appropriate to apply specific knowledge/skills in this new context. When students see that what they are learning can be applied to other contexts and real-life, their motivation and critical thinking are engaged.
Fail-Safe Strategies to try: • I Used to Think… But Now I Think… (page 136) • What? So What? Now What? (page 150)	Fail-Safe Strategies to try: • I Used to Think… But Now I Think… (page 136) • What? So What? Now What? (page 150)

• 3–2–1 Exit Card (page 139) • 5 W's and a How (page 142)	• 3–2–1 Exit Card (page 139) • 5 W's and a How (page 142) • What If…? (page 146)

How are these skills connected?

The process of drawing conclusions helps students identify and summarize key points worth remembering from the learning. It is an opportunity for students to communicate their understanding of scientific phenomena and principles. This new knowledge is then available to students to apply to new contexts when they see its relevance and a use for it.

CHAPTER 3

Introducing the Thinking Routines in the Classroom

Because the thinking routines will support students not only in science and language arts but also across the curriculum, it's essential that we get off to a strong start. Working with our teacher networks and in classrooms, we found that introducing each routine to students with a fun introductory lesson allowed us to dig deeper into the defining characteristics of the skills involved before layering in science content knowledge.

Consider introducing the thinking routines using the five lessons described below. We hope that these introductory lessons will create a sense of excitement and anticipation for upcoming activities and strategies. Every lesson includes an anchor chart that explains the thinking routine in student-friendly language to further support skill acquisition. Additionally, we have included an assessment tool, based on the anchor-chart criteria, that can be used by both teachers and students. Together, the lessons and assessment tools offer an introduction to the thinking routines.

Observe and Wonder: Missing Potato Report

Materials Needed

1 potato per student, measuring tapes/rulers, writing supplies (digital or paper)

Depending on class size, you could have one large pile or several smaller piles of potatoes in different locations in the room.

Students can use the chart in the Making Good Observations Assessment Tool on page 31 to make sure their list of observations meets as many criteria as possible.

1. Present the Making Good Observations anchor chart on page 30 for all to see. Explain that students will practice their observation skills using the criteria on the anchor chart. Let each student choose one potato from a pile.
2. Encourage students to describe their potato using the anchor chart tips. Observations can be recorded using a digital application or paper and pencil. Remind students that observations can be quantitative and qualitative.
3. Encourage pairs of students to review their list of observations and generate wonderings they might have about their partner's potato and its features. For example, students could wonder about the placement of eyes on the potato, variations in color, or identifying marks that make the potato unique. Prompt each student to return to their original list of observations and refine or add observations based on these wonderings. This is a great opportunity for students to distinguish and capture what makes their potato unique.
4. At this point it's critical to explain that, in science, a test of good observations is whether those observations can be replicated by someone else observing the

same situation. Tell students that, in order to test how good their observations are, they are going to use their observations to create a Missing Potato Report. Students can use the writing format of a detective's report, a Wanted poster, or a short story or poem to describe their potato. Creative writers might wish to create a context for how the potato went missing. Ask students to sign their report.

5. Redistribute finished reports to students in the classroom, ensuring no one gets their own. Place the potatoes back into a pile and challenge students to use the report they have to find the missing potato. Students can verify they have the correct potato by checking with the author of the original report.

Sample Missing Potato Report

Missing Potato Report

Ben, our classroom potato buddy, has gone missing from room 204! We are missing him and concerned due to the cold conditions here in Canada. He was last seen going to the cafeteria for a lunch break and hasn't returned since. We need your help in getting him back here a.s.a.p!

Description:
- Ben is 8 cm tall
- He has a tapered shape similar to a pear.
- His top is narrower than his bottom.
- He measures 2.5 cm on top with a circumference of 10 cm.
- He measures 4.5 cm on bottom with a circumference of 15.5 cm.
- He has a mass of 107 grams.
- Ben is light brown in appearance with some dark brown patches.
- While smooth in texture he does have many dimples or grooves – 21 to be exact.
- One groove in particular starts on the left about 2 cm down and continues to his middle where it meets a cut that resembles an eyebrow shape.
- Ben would fit into the palm of your hand.

If found please return to room 204! No questions will be asked.

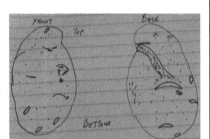

Making Good Observations

Observations need to be accurate and objective, so…

➤ use as many senses as possible, BUT never taste substances being used

➤ write down only what can be observed, not what you imagine is happening

➤ base observations on physical properties of matter; e.g., size, shape, color, odor, texture, density, solubility

➤ watch for changes over time

➤ use scientific language where you can

➤ include units of measurement, date, time

➤ draw and label a picture of what you observe

Pembroke Publishers ©2023 *Fail-Safe Strategies for Science and Literacy* by Sandra Mirabelli and Lionel Sandner ISBN 978-1-55138-364-4

Making Good Observations Assessment Tool

Did I…		
Use as many of my five senses as possible to describe the object or event?	Yes	No
Write down what I observed, not what I imagined?	Yes	No
Base my observations on physical properties of matter like size, shape, color, odor, texture, density, solubility?	Yes	No
Use scientific language where I could?	Yes	No
Watch for changes over time?	Yes	No
Include units of measurement, and the date and time observations were made?	Yes	No
Draw and label a picture of what I observed?	Yes	No

Extend Your Thinking

Was your missing potato found? What observations in your report did your partner say were most helpful in finding your potato?

Reflection

How could your report be improved?

Pembroke Publishers ©2023 *Fail-Safe Strategies for Science and Literacy* by Sandra Mirabelli and Lionel Sandner ISBN 978-1-55138-364-4

Activity adapted from Finson (2010)

Materials Needed

illustration of a tree with a squirrel holding a nut near the base, writing supplies (digital or paper)

Predict and Infer: Making Tree-mendous Inferences

1. Post an illustration of a tree and a squirrel for all to see. Details of the tree—like it having no leaves, roots exposed, and perhaps a broken branch—can expand the inferences possible. Also post the Making Good Inferences anchor chart on page 30.

2. Write the word *Observation* on a whiteboard, chart paper, or a digital tool; ask students to share what it means. Based on the Making Good Observations anchor chart on page 30, students might share, *Observations are information we can gather from an object or event based on our senses.*

3. Ask students to share what *inference* means. This time students might share the well-known language-arts formula: *It's a conclusion we draw based on information in the text and our background knowledge.* Reaffirm that this is correct. Clarify, however, that in science we make inferences based on our observations of a text and our scientific background knowledge. The text in science could be an experiment, a photo, etc. Also review that a prediction is a special type of inference about the future or what we think is going to happen.

4. Begin working with the tree illustration by asking students to predict why the squirrel might be at this tree. Students might offer, *Maybe the squirrel can store food there*, or *Maybe the squirrel is looking for a winter home.* Record these predictions on the board so they are visible to everyone.

5. Now prompt students to work with a partner and make observations based on the illustration. Create a T-chart with the heads *Observations* and *Inferences* to record students' observations. If students offer observations such as, *The tree is dead, hollow, large*, or *It's winter time*, be sure to point out that those are inferences rather than observations.

6. As a next step, guide students in making good inferences about the tree by grouping two or more observations from the class table together. For example, you might combine observations like *The tree has no leaves, there is a broken branch on the right, and the roots are exposed* to infer that *The tree is dead.* Write this inference in the Inferences column and indicate which observations were used to make it. For example, you might consider numbering the observations and noting which numbers were used. Provide time for students to combine other sets of observations and offer different inferences, such as *It's winter, The tree is old*, or *The tree is dead.*

7. Use the Making Good Inferences Assessment Tool on page 34 to reflect as a class on whether the inferences students have drawn meet the criteria outlined on the tool. Return to the initial predictions made by the class and discuss whether any observations confirm or refute the original predictions, or perhaps help make a better prediction about the squirrel's intentions.

Making Good Inferences

in•fer•ence: a conclusion or explanation made about an object or event based on observations. It is thinking beyond the information given to us.

Scientists combine their evidence (Observations) with what they already know about the world (Scientific Knowledge) to develop reasonable explanations (Inferences).

Observations + Scientific Knowledge = Inference

Remember, an inference…

➤ is only as good as the observations it is based on

➤ is only 1 of multiple possible explanations for a set of observations

➤ is not always correct

➤ is influenced by prior knowledge and experiences

Pembroke Publishers ©2023 *Fail-Safe Strategies for Science and Literacy* by Sandra Mirabelli and Lionel Sandner ISBN 978-1-55138-364-4

Making Good Inferences Assessment Tool

Did I...		
Use as many of my five senses as possible to describe the object or event?	Yes	No
Combine several observations together to make an inference?	Yes	No
Use my scientific knowledge to make a logical inference from the group of observations I combined together?	Yes	No
Use my real life experience(s) to help me make a good inference?	Yes	No

Extend Your Thinking

Give an example of several observations you combined together to make an inference. What was the inference you made as a result?

Reflection

What is the most important thing you learned about making good inferences? Explain why it is important.

Pembroke Publishers ©2023 *Fail-Safe Strategies for Science and Literacy* by Sandra Mirabelli and Lionel Sandner ISBN 978-1-55138-364-4

Sort and Categorize: Sort It Out

Materials Needed

objects to sort, writing supplies.

1. Invite students to share situations in real life where they had to sort a variety of objects. Encourage them to explain how they decided to do this task: e.g., laundry at home sorted by family member and type of item; clean kitchenware from the dishwasher sorted by the type of item and then the location in which it gets stored. Next, ask students to share why it is helpful to sort large groups of items.

2. Introduce the How to Sort and Categorize anchor chart on page 36. Prompt students to consider the collection of objects they have been provided with or brought in for this activity. Objects can be physical objects, such as a button collection, everyone's right shoe, or small puzzles of 50–100 pieces; groups of students could bring in collections from home if arranged beforehand; cards with pictures of objects would also work, e.g., a collection of emojis, different motor vehicles, or types of transportation. Give students time to discuss and sort their collections.

3. Ask students to work together to provide a label or category for each of the groupings they have created. They should also explain their thinking or sorting rule for each category. For example, with a puzzle, students might have grouped pieces together based on whether they were corner pieces, edge pieces, or middle pieces. They might explain that these groupings help with building the puzzle as they like to put the border together first.

Sorting a grouping further in this way reflects the structure of taxonomies in science, which students will encounter in biology.

4. Once groups have sorted their collections, prompt students to consider whether one grouping can be further sorted into subgroups. For example, the middle pieces of the puzzle could be sorted further by color or the object they are a part of.

5. Discuss the criteria in the Sort and Categorize Assessment Tool on page 37 with the class. Have students reflect on the groupings they have created with these criteria in mind. Students can then explore the different ways items have been sorted and categorized by students at other tables. As a class, discuss what they saw when visiting other tables and why categorizing or naming each group was helpful.

How to Sort and Categorize

| Sorting: | grouping items together because of similarities (e.g., size, shape, color, use, where found or kept) |

| Categorizing: | naming each group based on what is alike or common |

Graphic Organizers

that help us compare and contrast

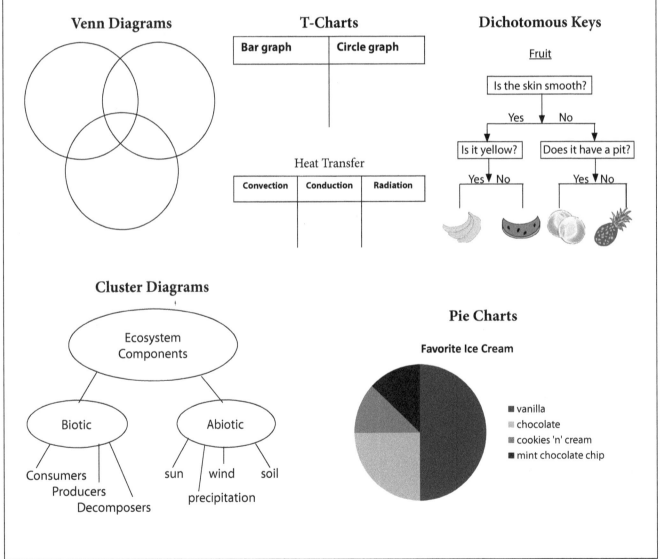

Venn Diagrams

T-Charts

Bar graph	Circle graph

Heat Transfer

Convection	Conduction	Radiation

Dichotomous Keys

Fruit

Is the skin smooth?

Yes   No

Is it yellow?   Does it have a pit?

Yes No   Yes No

Cluster Diagrams

Ecosystem Components

Biotic — Consumers, Producers, Decomposers

Abiotic — sun, wind, soil, precipitation

Pie Charts

Favorite Ice Cream

- vanilla
- chocolate
- cookies 'n' cream
- mint chocolate chip

Pembroke Publishers ©2023 *Fail-Safe Strategies for Science and Literacy* by Sandra Mirabelli and Lionel Sandner ISBN 978-1-55138-364-4

Sort and Categorize Assessment Tool

Did I…		
Sort a large group of objects into smaller groups based on similarities?	Yes	No
Ensure that my groupings were different from each other?	Yes	No
Provide a grouping rule to explain how I separated the larger collection into smaller groups?	Yes	No
Label each subset or smaller grouping with a category title?	Yes	No

Extend Your Thinking

What grouping rule(s) did you use to separate the larger collection into smaller groups?

Reflection

After looking at the grouping rules used by your classmates, how might you improve one of your rules? What might you do differently another time?

Pembroke Publishers ©2023 *Fail-Safe Strategies for Science and Literacy* by Sandra Mirabelli and Lionel Sandner ISBN 978-1-55138-364-4

Analyze and Interpret: Candy Kintsugi

Materials Needed

small packages of multi-colored candy (e.g., M&M's, Smarties, Skittles).
You may have pairs or groups of students bring in a small package of their own if there are any health concerns or protocols in the class/ school. However, it would be helpful for comparison and amalgamation of a larger set of data if the whole class works with the same type of candy.

An online search tells us that, on average, a package of M&M's milk chocolate candy should contain 24% blue, 20% orange, 16% green, 14% brown, 14% yellow, and 13% red. This data can be found online for many candy types.

Introducing the interpretation of the data in this way aligns with the *goal-free effect* (Paas, F. & Kirschner, F., 2012) in cognitive science where practicing problem-solving with a non-specific goal imposes a lower cognitive load on the novice problem-solver.

1. Use a visual example of a small puzzle depicting an animal or scenery to introduce the difference between analyzing and interpreting. Pull the puzzle pieces apart to illustrate that when we analyze something, we look at its individual parts to see how they relate to one another; when we interpret, we put all the pieces together again and tell the story of how everything fits together. Introduce the Analyze and Interpret anchor chart on page 39 as a support for this key difference.

2. Tell students that the class will practice these skills using candy. Inform them that they will have some time to work together to analyze their candy package and gather data. Invite students to share ideas about what kind of data they can collect; students might offer *the total number of candy pieces in the package, how many candies of each color are in the package, the number of whole pieces vs. the number of broken pieces.* As a class, decide what information everyone will collect. Provide chart paper and time for students to develop a graphic organizer to record this information.

3. Invite students to share their group data with the class. Begin to analyze the data by asking students to consider whether they notice any patterns or trends in the numbers (there are almost even numbers of each color of candy in each package) and whether anything is shocking or surprising (the number of candies in a package is not identical or it is identical).

4. Post the color distribution data for the type of candy the class has been working with. Work with students to consider how they can compare their own results to these percentages. Discuss the value of combining all group results into a class set before comparing. Provide time for students to work in their groups to collate data, determine percentages, and share their findings in the form of a graph. A conversation about the best type of graph would also be appropriate at this stage. This would highlight that either a pie or bar graph would be most beneficial for this data.

5. To move into the Interpret part of this thinking routine, explain that the Japanese art of *kintsugi* is the practice of fixing broken pottery by putting the pieces back together with gold, which highlights and enhances the pieces. Review the criteria presented in the Analyze and Interpret Assessment Tool on page 40 with the class to focus their attention on how they might think about the data they collected. Invite students to put the data about a package of candy back together better than before by sharing something they know now that they didn't know before about their package of candy.

6. It is important to remind students to use only the data in front of them (rather than searching online for further data) to make sense of it. Students might share things they found surprising (*their data did not match the company's color distribution information,* or *each package contained exactly the same amount of candy*). Prompt students to tell you more or tell why this could be, which could elicit further thinking; e.g., *maybe certain colors of dye have gone up in price or the resources needed to make them are not readily available so color distributions have changed; maybe consumer preferences or complaints have prompted the company to change color distributions; maybe each candy has the same mass so the company can weigh packages to ensure they contain the same amount of candy.* You might also consider having students think and write about what they know now, even before engaging in the class discussion. This type of writing to learn encourages students to synthesize information in novel ways before sharing ideas out loud.

Analyze and Interpret

Analyzing: breaking down a text or data into its parts, with the goal of finding patterns, trends, how things are related

Interpreting: putting the parts back together to logically explain what the patterns, trends, or relationships mean, with the goal of gaining insight and understanding

Ask:

- What does this data/text tell me?

- Is there anything missing?

- What does this all mean?

- What do I know now that I didn't know before?

Pembroke Publishers ©2023 *Fail-Safe Strategies for Science and Literacy* by Sandra Mirabelli and Lionel Sandner ISBN 978-1-55138-364-4

Analyze & Interpret Assessment Tool

Did I…		
Represent the data in different ways: e.g., tally, table, graph?	Yes	No
Look for patterns, trends, or relationships in the data?	Yes	No
Come up with logical explanations for what the data tells us or could mean?	Yes	No
Notice or learn something new about the object, situation, or event that I didn't know before?	Yes	No

Extend Your Thinking

Based on your analysis and interpretation of candy packaging, what is something you know now that you didn't know before?

Reflection

What is an important tip you could give a classmate to help them analyze and interpret data?

Pembroke Publishers ©2023 *Fail-Safe Strategies for Science and Literacy* by Sandra Mirabelli and Lionel Sandner ISBN 978-1-55138-364-4

Conclude and Apply: Sham-Wow!

Materials Needed

access to the ShamWow® infomercial (found online), writing supplies (paper or digital) for whole-class use

1. Prompt students to think about the informational writing they do and ask them to share what they include in their final paragraph—the conclusion. Students might share, *We revisit our main points in a brief way to summarize what we learned and what was important.* Ask students whether they think a conclusion in science does the same thing. Remind students that it is important to connect to scientific reasoning and principles when concluding a science report. Tell students that, in science, there is a framework we can use called Claims, Evidence, Reasoning (CER) that allows us to structure our thinking and write a conclusion. This framework is also helpful when examining other people's claims. Now you can introduce the Drawing Conclusions Using the CER Framework anchor chart on page 42.

2. Depending on the grade level, you might want to share some information about the CER framework to help them understand its purpose and value. The CER framework is useful for developing a supported argument when writing. It provides a structure for organizing sentences in a paragraph. The right side of the anchor chart outlines the steps we can use to do this. The CER framework is also useful for examining claims made in the media (Critical Media Literacy) and by news sources. This allows readers or viewers to assess whether a claim being made by someone is supported by evidence and reasoning. It also prompts the viewer to judge the quality of that evidence and reasoning. The left side of the anchor chart guides us through this process.

3. Let students know that in this lesson the class will deconstruct a popular infomercial using the CER framework. Emphasize that you will use the left side of the anchor chart—*When reading, look for*—to help you do this.

4. Invite students to watch the original version of the ShamWow® infomercial and listen for the reasons the sales agent in the commercial, Vince, says we should buy a ShamWow® towel; *Buy a ShamWow™ cloth because you'll say "Wow" every time you use it*; in other words, because it is really good. Identify this as the *claim* being made.

5. Have students watch the infomercial again, this time listening carefully to the *evidence* the sales agent provides to support his claim. You might need to replay this portion of the video several times. Debrief with students by recording the evidence they pick out of the video: *it holds 20 times its weight in moisture; it lasts 10 years; it will save you $20 per month in paper towels; it's made by the Germans and Germans make good stuff; Olympic divers use it; it acts like a vacuum to soak up spills.*

Reviewing the criteria on the Conclude and Apply Assessment Tool on page 43 with students and discussing the presence or absence of each item in a text will help the class determine what could strengthen a conclusion or argument.

6. Now encourage students to consider whether the evidence presented supports the claim being made. Point out that providing the scientific *reasoning* behind why the towel works so well would strengthen the reasoning and provide a powerful conclusion to the infomercial. Explain that, while the infomercial hasn't given us this scientific reasoning, we can search for it. Have the class consider a cloth like the ShamWow® they might have at home. Students might say that they have used microfibre cloths to pick up dust or clean up spills. As a class, an online search for "how microfibre cloth works" or the "science of tiny threads" will help students gain the scientific knowledge needed to better evaluate the evidence and the claim. This will help them draw a strong conclusion and decide whether to believe the claim.

Drawing Conclusions Using the CER Framework

When reading, look for…		When writing…
A statement presented as truth	the **CLAIM**	Use words and ideas from the question to provide a direct response.
The information or data used to back up the claim that is made: • Is it valid? • Is it reliable?	the **EVIDENCE**	Present reliable information (data and observations) that support the claim: "According to…" "The data shows…" "One piece of evidence is…"
An explanation of how or why the evidence supports the claim: • Are related scientific terms and principles presented?	the **REASONING**	Explain how or why the evidence supports the claim. Include related scientific terms and principles: "Based on the evidence…" "This confirms that…"

Pembroke Publishers ©2023 *Fail-Safe Strategies for Science and Literacy* by Sandra Mirabelli and Lionel Sandner ISBN 978-1-55138-364-4

Conclude and Apply Assessment Tool

Did I…		
Answer the focus question by identifying a claim or the claim being made?	Yes	No
Gather evidence that supports the claim?	Yes	No
Identify a scientific principle or knowledge connected to this object or phenomenon?	Yes	No
Explain how the scientific principle or knowledge is the reason this evidence allows for this claim to be made?	Yes	No

Extend Your Thinking

What might you suggest the creators of ShamWow® include in their commercial to improve their sales pitch?

Reflection

Think of a situation in or out of school where a claim was made. What evidence and reasoning did you use to determine if the claim was believable?

CHAPTER 4

Fail-Safe Strategies

The Fail-Safe Strategies presented in this book are designed to help students think deeply about the concepts behind the science activities and gain practice in using the thinking routines while applying them in different contexts. They provide a structure that helps students develop the knowledge and habits needed to succeed in science.

You might already recognize many of the strategies in this book as literacy, learning, or assessment strategies. Essentially, each of the Fail-Safe Strategies fosters a particular way of thinking about the phenomenon in the science activity by applying a literacy lens. As Fisher, Frey and Hattie (2016) point out, "Literacy is great at teaching you how to think successively—that is, making meaning one step at a time to then build a story." Applying a literacy lens provides students with another entry point into learning about complex concepts in science. The Fail-Safe Strategies are designed to ensure all students are able to participate in scientific inquiry and experimentation, regardless of their prior knowledge or background. Students use the Fail-Safe Strategies as a short-term support for their thinking until, with practice, they develop and automatize the skills and processes as thinking routines.

Building the thinking routines by using the Fail-Safe Strategies is critical for students for several reasons:

- By directing students' attention, the strategies encourage them to actively think about content or a text in an intentional and thoughtful way (Shanahan, T., 2022; Duke, N. K., Ward, A. E., Pearson, P. D., 2021).
- We know that when "students don't have much knowledge of the strategies they might employ to facilitate and direct their thinking… they are likely to be less effective, less independent, less engaged, and less metacognitive" (Ritchhart, R., Church, M., Morrison, K., 2011).
- Cognitive science reminds us that the brain is a natural pattern-seeker (Zadina, J., 2014). The Fail-Safe Strategies slow down students' thinking to ensure students stay focused for a longer period of time on parts of an activity or text that they might have otherwise ignored or overlooked. The strategies work to distract the brain from its natural tendency to quickly interpret and possibly jump to inaccurate conclusions (Kahneman, D., 2011).

- We recognize an added benefit that comes with the deliberate and repeated use of the Fail-Safe Strategies: this type of thinking will become more automatic over time, reducing students' cognitive load and freeing up working memory to focus on other aspects of a task or phenomenon (see page 16).

Educators can also use our Fail-Safe Strategies to guide small-group and whole-class discussions. The strategies make students' thinking visible through oral, written, and visual means. This will allow you to lead a productive discussion, guiding students to clarify their thinking and push it to deeper levels so that they can make sense of the science concept(s) featured in the activity.

Another key part of strategy use in the classroom is discussing the effectiveness of the strategy with students after the science activity to support students in cognition (acquiring knowledge and understanding of science and literacy concepts) and metacognition (thinking about and monitoring their thinking) in their journey to becoming self-regulated learners (see *germane load* on page 17). Discussing the effectiveness of the strategy with students after the activity helps students reflect on their own learning process. This will empower them to better understand how and when to use the strategy to enhance their thinking and understanding.

Perspective feature by Lionel Sandner

Why Science Activities?

I remember thinking, the night before my first day of teaching, about what would be the first science activity I could do to engage the students. The original idea that was shared with my class and professor during teacher ed training seemed rather lame. And this was before the days of the Internet and its wealth of ideas. I found a book on science demonstrations in the library; buried deep in the pages was an activity called "The Egg in the Cup." It seemed like a perfect fit. All I needed was a coffee cup, a spool of thread, a cookie sheet, an egg, and a broom. I had all those materials, so I was good to go. It took a few tries and a broken egg or two, but it turned out to be a very cool demonstration, both at home when I practiced and the next day in class. At that moment, I realized the power a science activity could have in engaging students.

You can find the Egg in the Cup demonstration as Activity #10 in this book. I have used this activity many times as an introduction to my classes, workshops, and presentations. And each time I do it, I learn something new about science, people, and human behavior. Science is the study of our world and the collection of evidence to explain how it works. That's a hefty task, but a process that provides the foundation for lifelong learning. I believe it's impossible not to be curious and experience the amazing wonder of our universe when you learn something new about the world around you. Age doesn't matter and anyone can start at any time to explore and gain a better understanding of why something happens. That's why the 25 activities in this book provide a foundation for you to bring into your classroom. Most activities don't require any special equipment; they just require you to do what I did the first time. Try it at home, and if it brings a smile or joy to your heart, try it with your class. My vision is that every teacher should be able to do these 25 science activities and combine them with our thinking routines.

As I reflect on my science experiences during my teaching career, several themes emerge that I think you may find helpful to remember. The list is not exhaustive, but if you can remember them, it will help guide you.

Remember Safety

In any science activity, the safety of you and your students is paramount. If you are unsure, always ask for guidance. While each educational system is different, there are always safety consultants, colleagues, and community experts who can provide support. There might be safety policies that can also provide guidance. Several of the activities in this book require an open flame. Balancing the risk of the activity with the learning experience is always one of the decisions you must make as a professional when you're lesson planning. The National Science Teachers Association (nsta.org) has many resources to support safety when teaching science. The best motto to keep in mind is *When in doubt, ask.* And as a corollary, ask for safety training in areas where you are unsure.

Ask Why

In any science endeavor, there will be an opportunity to ask *Why?* This is the perfect opportunity to expand curiosity and students' interest to explore further. It's that moment when you sense the class wondering how the activity worked that you can build the motivation and engagement to go further into understanding the science. That is the power of the Egg in the Cup activity. Everyone wants to know how it happened. Everyone wants to know why.

Take Intellectual Risks

Once safety concerns are addressed, there is ample room to demonstrate the importance of taking intellectual risks. This is an important theme to remember when doing any science activity. If students observe you trying something new, then they are more apt to try it themselves in a different learning context. The Egg in the Cup activity brings the element of risk into the activity with the possibility of the egg breaking. Believe it or not, this immediately focuses people of any age to become engaged and begin to predict what will happen. At that point, let the learning begin.

Accept that Things Don't Always Go as Planned

Sometimes an activity doesn't quite work as you expect. That's okay, and part of the learning experience. There is no rule that says an activity can be done only once. Sometimes the best learning comes when you examine, reflect why something didn't work, and try again. There are times when the Egg in the Cup activity doesn't work, and those tend to prompt the most interesting conversations with students. Building on the ideas from a debrief leads to repeating the activity successfully.

As part of your debrief of an activity and Fail-Safe Strategy pairing, consider leading a discussion and asking

- *Was the Fail-Safe Strategy we used today helpful?*
- *Did it allow you to see or think in a new or different way?*
- *Was it helpful in prompting the kind of thinking we focused on today?*
- *Would it support any of the other thinking routines we are practicing?*
- *When else might we use this strategy?*

Our goal as educators is for students to select and apply the appropriate Fail-Safe Strategy because they realize the strategies develop their literacy skills while they think more deeply about the science concepts and phenomena we are studying.

Using the Fail-Safe Strategies

As you look through the 25 Fail-Safe Strategies you'll notice there is a common framework of three components: the Strategy, the Science Activity, and one or more student-friendly organizers. Here's a quick overview of each section in the activity.

The Strategy

There isn't any particular order to the activities presented in this book. We have, however, paired each Fail-Safe Strategy with a science activity based on the content to be learned and the thinking routine we set out to develop. Many of the science activities could be done with other strategies to develop other thinking routines. Once you become comfortable with this set of Fail-Safe Strategies, you can find different combinations that engage students with the science content in a meaningful way as they work toward automatizing the thinking routines.

Every strategy identifies

- the thinking routine that will be activated,
- a suggested pairing with a science activity from the book
- the phase of the activity (before, during, or after the activity) in which the strategy is introduced and used

The Fail-Safe Strategy template also describes

- the purpose for using this literacy strategy with science content
- how the Fail-Safe Strategy is be carried out with the corresponding science activity during science time
- helpful tips, suggested prompts, and modifications for using the Fail-Safe Strategy with the selected science activity
- suggestions for instruction during language-arts time to build background knowledge and to foster familiarity with related science concepts and vocabulary, and with the Fail-Safe Strategy itself

Because we understand that the background knowledge and vocabulary students bring influences comprehension, we have included two special features to support you in this area.

- The ABCs of Background Knowledge feature activates a key concept related to the focus science activity. A student-friendly definition is provided to help build background knowledge of the concept while an explanation of the connection to the science activity helps lay the groundwork for more in-depth learning and schema connection.
- The Vocabulary Spotlight highlights key terms and academic language related to the focus science activity. When students learn about word origins and morphology, it helps them better understand scientific terminology, while developing the language foundations they need for reading and writing. The process of studying word parts, such as prefixes, root words or bases, and suffixes, expands students' vocabulary and improves their ability to pronounce and predict the meaning of new and unfamiliar words.

The Student-Friendly Organizers

A strategy organizer (or more than one) customized for each Fail-Safe Strategy and science activity pairing is provided to scaffold students' use of the strategy. As a process piece, the strategy organizer allows students to organize and document their ideas and thinking, and to make it visible to you. It also allows you, the educator, to track students' understanding of a concept, pinpoint areas of difficulty or misconceptions, and adjust instruction accordingly.

The Science Activity

Embedded in each Fail-Safe Strategy is a suggested science activity to pair it with. Each activity includes

- Summary: a brief description of the activity
- Hints: one or more suggestions to help perform the activity
- Explanation: notes on the science content that can be introduced and explored by doing the activity
- Supplies: a list of materials needed to perform the activity. Amounts of each supply have been done in common household measurements to simplify preparation. The amounts are for one activity. If individual students are doing the activity, multiply amounts accordingly.
- Safety: special considerations related to safety, an icon, and information
- Directions: step-by-step instructions on how to perform the activity
- QR Code: scan the code to link to a short video of the activity being done.

Fire Safety

Safety

Safe Disposal

Notes about Safety and Disposal

Safety

When performing any science activity, ensure you are following your school board's safety policies. The National Science Teachers Association (nsta.org) is an excellent resource. Several of the activities require an open flame, and it is essential that you ensure the safety of your students and yourself. Follow all policies related to fire safety in your school.

Safe Disposal

Most activities use materials purchased at a grocery store or pharmacy. Follow directions on the label for safe disposal. Any special disposal considerations will be noted in the activity.

Balancing Learning Risk with Learning Opportunities

Many science safety policies acknowledge the need to balance learning risk with learning opportunity for the student. In deciding to do an activity like Kissing Candles (Activity #5), it's important to consider how the activity will support student learning while maintaining a safe classroom environment. There may be situations where it is appropriate to do the activity as a demo rather than have students do the activity on their own or in groups. And this can change from year to year. Llewellyn (2002) provides a good list of considerations to use when deciding if the activity should be teacher-led. An activity should be teacher-led if

- all students need to observe a particular phenomenon
- the procedure is too complicated for students to follow
- the results of the situation need to be controlled
- dangerous, toxic, or flammable materials are used
- safety is a concern
- materials or equipment are limited
- expensive chemicals or supplies are being used
- time is of the essence

While this list is not exhaustive, it provides a good starting point for considering how you use any science activity in your class. Remember: If you don't know, ask.

PART 2

The Fail-Safe Strategies

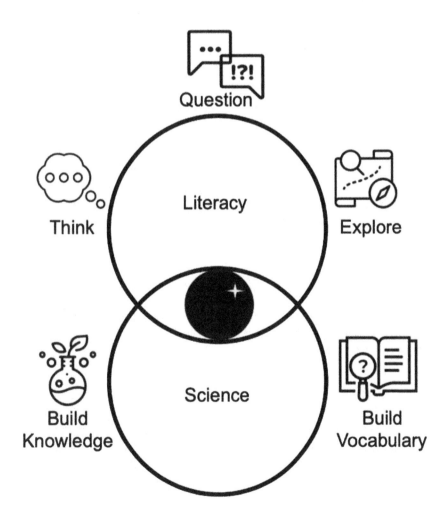

Fail-Safe Strategies and Activities at a Glance

Science Activity	Literacy Strategy	Science Concept
Thinking Routine: Observe & Wonder		
Drops of Water on a Coin, page 57	1. See, Think, Wonder, page 54 • Connect to prior knowledge • Spark curiosity • Generate wonderings	**Properties of Water:** Water is "sticky" because of the cohesive and adhesive forces between molecules. • You can put more drops than expected on the coin because of the stickiness of water.
Dancing Raisins, page 62	2. Wait … What?, page 58 • Slow down looking • Look beyond the obvious • Look at finer details	**Chemical Change:** a change in which one or more new substances are formed; e.g. baking soda and vinegar form carbon dioxide • Carbon dioxide bubbles act as flotation devices for raisins.
Can You Lift This?, page 67	3. Before and After Diagrams, page 63 • Enhance explanations • Track changes in the phenomenon observed • Make student thinking and mental models visible through visuals	**Friction:** when an object rubs against another, creating resistance to motion • Pencil movement up and down on the rice compacts the rice.
Candy Color Wheel, page 70	4. Think, Question, Explore, page 68 • Think about what is already known • Identify questions of interest to explore	**Diffusion:** a mixing process where the particles of one substance spread out in the particles of another substance • As the food dye dissolves into water, the color spreads out because of diffusion.
Kissing Candles, page 73	5. Q-Chart Question Prompts, page 71 • Generate large volume and variety of questions of personal interest • Expand range of questions from closed to open and divergent	**Convection Currents:** the cycle created when heated molecules in a fluid rise and then sink as they cool • Air rises from the heat of the candle flame. Cooler air rushes in from below the flame to create the convection current.
Thinking Routine: Predict and Infer		
Inference Cube, page 76	6. Inference Ladder, page 74 • Slow down thinking • Select and interpret observations to arrive at a logical conclusion	**Models/Black Box:** a physical or visual representation of an idea, process, or system that helps describe a phenomenon in the natural world that we can't experience directly • By collecting evidence of patterns, we can infer what is on the side that we can't see.
Inference Can, page 79	7. Think, Pair, Share, Draw, page 77 • Provide individual think time for better quality initial responses • Collaborate with peers to refine thinking • Draw model to make thinking visible	**Inference:** a conclusion you make based on evidence and background knowledge • The skill of inferring is used across the curriculum to think beyond a text or about an object or event in the natural world.

Geyser in a Bottle, page 84	8. Trending Now, page 80 • Predict the outcome of an activity • Use descriptive language to capture audience attention and build anticipation	**Physical Change:** a change in size, shape, appearance, state of matter; the substance does not become a different substance • The carbon dioxide in the diet soda phase-changes to a gas when it comes in contact with the candy; the physical change happens rapidly and creates a fountain effect.
Piercing Pencils, page 88	9. Predict, Explain, Observe, Explain, page 85 • Make a prediction based on prior knowledge and explain it • Gather and interpret data to revisit the prediction and draw a conclusion	**Plastic:** human-made material composed of polymers or long repeating chains of molecules • The pencil pushes the polymer strands apart and creates space for it to penetrate the plastic bag.
Egg in a Cup, page 92	10. Poll Everyone, page 89 • Predict the outcome based on background knowledge and previous experience • Share predictions and look for patterns in responses	**Newton's First Law of Motion:** An object will stay at rest or in motion until an outside force starts it moving, speeds it up, slows it down, or changes its direction of movement. • The egg's inertia keeps it in place until a force removes the cookie sheet and spool of thread from underneath it. Then gravity overcomes the egg's inertia and it falls in the cup.

Thinking Routine: Sort and Categorize

Crushed Can, page 97	11. Question Sorter, page 93 • Consider 3 types of questions encountered in science: testable, researchable, ponderable • Gain insight into what is involved in answering these questions	**Pressure:** the amount of force exerted on an area • Boiling water in the can and flipping it over into ice water lowers the pressure inside the can, causing pressure outside the can to implode it.
Cheese Stick Candle, page 100	12. Chain Notes, page 98 • Add new ideas, facts, examples to class notes • Build one another's ideas with new connections	**Observations:** looking closely to describe an object, situation, or event • Observations might cause students to incorrectly infer the composition of the candle.
Reaction in a Bag, page 103	13. List–Group–Label, page 101 • Organize content-specific vocabulary prior to activity • Connect to prior knowledge • Anticipate new learning	**Chemical Reaction:** a chemical change that results in new substances being made • The evidence of new substances being created in the plastic bag is the feeling of warmth (exothermic) or cold (endothermic).
Static Action, page 107	14. Visual Word Sort, page 104 • Activate prior knowledge • Become familiar with vocabulary • Revisit vocabulary to track new learning	**Static Charge:** an imbalance of electric charges on the surface of a material or between materials • The static charge on the balloon induces a charge on the gelatin, causing it to stand up.
What's in a Mixture?, page 114	15. GO with the Flow, page 108 • Select most appropriate graphic organizer to represent ideas • Collaborate with a peer to examine similarities and differences	**Separation Techniques:** the process of separating out different materials • The separation of the mechanical mixture requires the use of separation techniques, including hand-picking, dissolving, evaporation, filtration, magnetism.

Thinking Routine: Analyze and Interpret		
Paper Pot, page 118	16. What Makes You Say That?, page 115 • Invite students to elaborate on their responses • Encourage students to support responses with evidence and reasoning	**Heat Transfer:** the movement of thermal energy from an area of warm to cool • Thermal energy from the flame transfers to the paper and then to the water. The paper never gets hot enough to burn.
Flying Teabag, page 122	17. Connect Two, page 119 • Look for similarities and differences to connect concepts • Search for patterns and relationships between concepts	**Temperature:** degree of hotness or coldness of an object measured on a scale; the average moving (kinetic) energy of particles within a system • Lighting the teabag increases the temperature and the resulting heat makes air particles move faster and spread further apart, creating less-dense air. The convection current causes the last piece of the tea bag to rise.
Glowing Spice, page 125	18. Take Note, page 123 • Identify key learning and questions • Analyze confusing and challenging parts of an activity	**Chemiluminescence:** the emission of light during a chemical reaction. • The UV light energy interacts with the turmeric, causing the spice to glow.
How Big? How Small?, page 130	19. 3-D GO, page 126 • Create a 3-D interactive graphic organizer • Chunk information for note-taking	**Unit:** a standard measurement of physical quantities of the same kind • Use prefixes as a short-hand method for identifying very large and very small things.
A Busy Cup of Science, page 135	20. Frayer Model, page 132 • Build a deeper understanding of key vocabulary • Outline key characteristics, examples, and non-examples	**Density:** a measurement of how tightly materials are packed together • Vegetable oil floats on water because it is less dense.
Thinking Routine: Conclude and Apply		
Toilet Paper Rope, page 138	21. I Used to Think… But Now I Think… , page 136 • Reflect on learning • Look for how and why perceptions or beliefs have changed	**Physical Properties:** characteristics that enable us to differentiate one material from another • Modifications to the properties of a material can create novel uses. • Layering and twisting toilet paper creates a rope.
Water Screen, page 141	22. 3–2–1 Exit Card, page 139 • Summarize learning • Identify areas of interest and further questions	**Properties of Water:** Water's high surface tension causes the outer layer to act like a skin. • The high surface tension of water combined with the small holes in the mesh prevent water from going through.
Better Paper Towel, page 145	23. 5 W's and a How, page 142 • Create questions to gather information for problem-solving • Draw conclusions from findings • Apply learning to establish significance	**Properties of Water:** Capillary action lets liquid flow into narrow spaces without the assistance of force, because of cohesion, adhesion, and surface tension. • By folding the paper towel, spaces are created between the layers to hold water.

How Do You Know It's Fair?, page 149	24. What If…, page 146 • Think about cause-and-effect relationships • Look for new or different ways to do things	**Dissolving:** the process in which a solute forms a solution with another substance, the solvent • A candy dissolves in your mouth because the sugar (the solute) combines with the saliva (the solvent) to create a sugar solution.
Iodine Clock, page 153	25. What? So What? Now What?, page 150 • Engage in reflective thinking • Consider implications and importance of results • Consider how new knowledge might be applied in problem-solving	**Rates of Reaction:** Chemical reactions can be fast or slow, and the rate can depend on factors like temperature, concentration, and surface area. • The iodine clock reaction can vary in time by changing the temperature of the starting materials.

See, Think, Wonder

Strategy Connections

Thinking Routine: Observe and Wonder
Science Activity: Drops of Water on a Coin, page 57
When to Use: During the activity
After the activity

The See, Think, Wonder strategy (adapted from Ritchart et. al., 2011) encourages students to look closely as they make observations about what they see during an activity or demonstration. Asking students what they think about what they've seen prompts them to connect to prior knowledge and to begin to search for significance in what they observed. Starting with students' observations sparks their curiosity and will help them generate wonderings about the materials, procedures, and larger contexts surrounding the phenomenon being observed.

Using the Strategy with the Drops of Water on a Coin Activity

During Science Time

- Once materials for Drops of Water on a Coin (page 57) are distributed, pose the question,

  How many drops of water do you think you can fit on the coin?

  Post student predictions for the whole class to see.
- Have the Making Good Observations anchor chart on page 30 visible as a support for students. As students work in pairs, encourage them to ensure one partner is recording their observations as the other partner places drops of water on the coin. Prompt students to make observations by describing the materials. Ask: *What do you see?* Extend this to ask *Why do you think this is happening?* Provide time for students to record these observations on the See, Think, Wonder strategy organizer on page 56.
- Remind students to count the drops of water that fit on the coin so they can revisit the opening question and their predictions. The number of drops that can be held on the coin becomes a quantitative observation students can add to their list of observations. Encourage students to include a labelled diagram of the phenomenon in the space provided on the organizer. Invite students to share how many drops of water they were able to fit on the coin before water began to spill over the sides. Record these numbers for the whole class to see.
- After the activity, ask students to think about and use their scientific knowledge and experience of water to consider why the water behaved in this way: *The separate drops joined together to form a larger bubble-shaped drop on the coin.*

  Provide time for students to record their thinking on the strategy organizer and share some possibilities aloud with the whole class.
- Prompt students to revisit their thinking and consider why there was a variation in the number of drops of water that different groups fit on their coin and how they could fit more drops of water on the coin. At this point, it might be helpful to provide this sentence stem—"*I wonder if we…*—to prompt their wondering: *I wonder if we could fit more drops of water on the coin if we used the other side of the coin? Or if we used a different liquid? Or if we held the dropper closer to the surface of the coin?*

Provide time for the pairs to record their wonderings on their strategy organizer.

Variations/Tips/Useful Prompts

In order to guide students as they are observing in science, encourage them to

- Describe the size, shape, and/or color of the object(s) being viewed. In the Drops of Water on a Coin activity, students may describe the placement of the water on the coin and observe the water from both side and top views.
- Consider whether any of the properties of the material(s) change throughout the activity
- Consider what you are doing with materials and equipment during this activity; for example, students will want to look at how large the drops of water are and how high above the coin the dropper is held.

When generating wonderings, encourage students to

- Look back at their observations as a starting point for generating questions.
- Consider question words they might use to start wonderings; e.g., *What if... ? How would... ? Why...?*
- Use the Q-Chart on page 72 to generate more questions.

During Language-Arts Time

Have students practice using the See, Think, Wonder strategy with a variety of visual texts, including picture books, art pieces, and media texts. Post a digital or paper version of the See, Think, Wonder strategy organizer on page 56 for all to see. Record class ideas on the See, Think, Wonder organizer and remind students to refer back to responses in other boxes as they practice using the strategy.

Use questions to review the key words and provide some alternatives to expand student thinking:

- *What do you see, notice or observe in this text?*
- *What does this make you think will happen? What has happened?*
- *What wonderings or questions do you have about what has happened or will happen next? Is there anything that surprises you? Is there anything you find mysterious?*

The ABCs of Background Knowledge *(Activate, Build, Connect)*	Vocabulary Spotlight
Properties of Water: Water is considered sticky because of the cohesive and adhesive forces between water molecules. • The ability to add more drops to the coin than expected is caused by the stickiness of water.	*Cohesion; Adhesion* • Root word *hesion* means "to stick"; prefix *ad–* means "toward"; prefix *co–* means "with; together; jointly" • Related words: adhesive, adhere

See, Think, Wonder

See

Record your observations in the space below. Remember to document what you see, not what you think is happening. Include a labelled diagram of the water on the coin. Can you include any measurements?

Think

Why do you think you were able to fit so many drops of water on the coin? Explain your thinking. Use your scientific knowledge and experience with water to help you.

Wonder

Were you surprised by what happened? Or that other groups were able to fit even more drops of water on the coin? How could you fit more drops of water on your coin? Consider how you could change the materials or the procedure for this activity. Record these ideas as wonderings below.

Pembroke Publishers ©2023 *Fail-Safe Strategies for Science and Literacy* by Sandra Mirabelli and Lionel Sandner ISBN 978-1-55138-364-4

Drops of Water on a Coin

Students use an eyedropper to put drops of water on a coin. During this activity, they test their prediction of how many drops of water can be placed on the coin. This activity can be extended to a discussion on conducting a fair test (see Activity #24) and on identifying and controlling variables. Or it can be used to help students develop their observation skills.

Hint

- Fold paper towel in half or quarters to help absorb any spilled water.

Explanation

This activity is called a *discrepant event*, as most predictions underestimate the number of drops that will fit on a coin. This is because the predictions do not take into account the cohesive nature of water. Water molecules have a natural cohesion or attraction to other water molecules. When water is dropped on a coin, the molecules stick to each other and create a dome shape on the coin instead of rolling off it. This allows for more water drops to be placed on the coin than originally expected.

Supplies

- coin
- eye dropper
- small cup
- water
- paper towel

Directions

1. Each student or group receives a coin, cup, eye dropper, and paper towel.
2. Half fill the cup with water.
3. Predict how many drops of water can be placed on the coin.
4. Test your prediction by adding drops of water on the coin. While doing the test, write down three to five observations and wonderings.
5. Compare predictions to actual results and discuss what factors (variables) influenced results.
6. Repeat test while controlling identified variables.
7. Compare results and complete the See, Think, Wonder strategy organizer.

STRATEGY #2
Wait... What?

Strategy Connections

Thinking Routine: Observe and Wonder
Science Activity: Dancing Raisins, page 62
When to Use: Before the activity
During the activity
After the activity

The Wait... What? strategy encourages students to slow down while observing a phenomenon in science. By having to record a first set of observations and then look again to generate a second set of different observations, students move beyond the obvious and look more closely for finer details they may not have noticed at first.

Using the Strategy with the Dancing Raisins Activity

During Science Time

- Prompt students to look at the materials (the dry raisins) to be used in the Dancing Raisins activity on page 62 before they are added to the beaker. Have students record their observations about the dry raisins on the Wait... What? Observations strategy organizer on page 60. For example, they might write, *The raisins are dark brown, they are rough in texture or wrinkly, they are round.* As materials (water, baking soda) are added into the beaker, students can add a few more observations about the solution being created to the first set of boxes on the strategy organizer. For example, students might add, *The baking soda is dissolving.*

- For the second set of observations, prompt students to add the raisins to the water and baking soda solution. Once the vinegar is added, the raisins will begin to move. Prompt students with the phrase "Wait ... What?" as a signal that they need to look more closely at what is happening to the materials now that they are all combined. Students can now generate a new set of observations. These observations can be recorded in the second set of boxes on the Wait... What? Observations strategy organizer. For example, students might write, *Tiny bubbles are forming on the raisins, some raisins are floating to the top of the beaker, the raisins sink again very quickly.* Have students share their lists of observations and discuss whether each group saw the same things happening.

Variations/Tips/Useful Prompts

- For the first set of observations, encourage students to record first impressions and broad observations. Prompt students to consider the physical properties of the raisins being used in the activity. They can describe size, shape, color, and texture.

- The second set of observations require students to look more closely at a phenomenon. Usually the "Wait... What?" prompt is best offered when a change begins in the investigation or when something surprising or unexpected begins to happen. In the Dancing Raisins activity (page 62), you can support closer looking by posing questions; e.g., *What might be causing the raisins to "dance" or rise in the beaker? Why do you think some raisins sink back down in the beaker?* In this way, you support students in looking more closely to see what could be contributing to this movement. For example, students might notice that the bubbles of carbon dioxide burst once the raisins reach the top of the liquid, and then the raisins sink to the bottom again.

During Language-Arts Time

Good observations and the use of sketches and measurements are helpful in a variety of fields, including science and geography. In some cases, they are a form of research (e.g., Jane Goodall's work with chimpanzees in the wild) on their own. Good observations can help scientists make better predictions and inferences about future events. Good observations also help scientists understand and explain phenomena better. Review the Making Good Observations anchor chart from The Missing Potato lesson on page 30. We can support students in making good observations by considering three ways that grammar can help us make our vocabulary more descriptive and precise when describing an object or event.

1. As a starting point, have students generate a list of words other than *walk* to describe how someone could move down a hallway in the school. Discuss how words—*strolled, ambled*—or a phrase like *aimlessly wandered* more precisely describe movement. Explain that sometimes more vivid action words or a short phrase help paint a better picture of what is happening.

2. Using the online search phrases "microscopic close-up of raisins" or "food under the microscope: raisins" find a good photo to post for the class to see. Use this image as a focus for instruction as students work through the Wait… What? Language strategy organizer on page 61. Prompt students to consider how we use adjectives to describe nouns. What adjectives other than *dark* or *wavy* could be used to better describe the object in the photo? Working with a partner, students can continue to create short lists of adjectives that would describe the size, shape, color, and texture of the object in the picture. You can later reveal the identity of the object they are viewing; it is an image of a dry raisin under a microscope.

3. Lastly, remind students that adverbs are used to describe verbs. What adverbs might we use to describe the movement of an object; e.g., a bird moving through the sky? Using adverbs can help paint a better picture of speed and direction or of the pathway of movement. Thinking about how adverbs are used to describe verbs will support students in making good observations, once the raisins are added to the liquid in the Dancing Raisins activity (page 62).

The ABCs of Background Knowledge *Activate, Build, Connect*	Vocabulary Spotlight
Chemical Change: a change in which one or more new substances are formed; e.g., baking soda and vinegar form carbon dioxide. • Carbon dioxide bubbles act as flotation devices on raisins.	*Buoyant* • Root word *buoy* means "having the ability to float" • Related words: buoyancy, buoy *Carbon Dioxide (CO_2)* • Prefix *di–* in dioxide means "two, twice, double"; *dioxide* indicates something has 2 oxygen atoms • Related word: oxide

Wait… What?
Observations

Looking Closely

Record a first set of observations before the activity: Dry Raisins

1	
2	
3	
4	
5	
6	
7	

Looking More Closely

Record another set of observations during and after the activity: Wet Raisins

1	
2	
3	
4	
5	
6	
7	

Pembroke Publishers ©2023 *Fail-Safe Strategies for Science and Literacy* by Sandra Mirabelli and Lionel Sandner ISBN 978-1-55138-364-4

Wait… What?
Language

Describing Nouns with Adjectives

Use the box below to add as many adjectives as you can to describe what you see in the photo that has been posted by your teacher. Think about adjectives you can use to describe color, shape, size, and texture.

Describing Verbs with Adverbs

Find a short video clip of a bird or other animal moving through a habitat. Record adverbs that describe the speed, direction, and/or pathway of the animal's movement.

Pembroke Publishers ©2023 *Fail-Safe Strategies for Science and Literacy* by Sandra Mirabelli and Lionel Sandner ISBN 978-1-55138-364-4

Dancing Raisins

After creating a diluted, carbonated solution of 50% water, 50% acetic acid (vinegar), and a tablespoon of baking soda in a clear cup, dry raisins are added. The raisins sink to the bottom, then begin to rise to the surface and fall back down. This process can last from several minutes to a half hour.

Hints

- Add acid to water.
- Slowly add baking soda to prevent overflow of solution.
- The drier the raisins, the better.

Explanation

The dry raisins sink to the bottom because they are denser than the carbonated solution. The bubbles are carbon dioxide, and they stick to the wrinkled surface of each raisin. When enough bubbles attach to a raisin, the overall density of the raisin is reduced to less than the density of the water. This causes the raisin to rise to the surface. At the surface, the carbon dioxide bubbles are released into the atmosphere and the raisins sink to the bottom.

Supplies

- water (approximately 125 ml/½ cup)
- vinegar (approximately 125 ml/½ cup)
- baking soda (approximately 10 g/1 tablespoon)
- measuring spoon
- clear cup or 400 ml beaker
- paper towel

Directions

1. Pour 125 ml/½ cup of water into the container.
2. Place 10 g/1 tablespoon of baking soda into the container and stir until baking soda is dissolved.
3. Place the container on a plate or baking pan (in case of spillage).
4. Slowly add 125 ml/½ cup vinegar to container.
5. Place raisins in container and observe.
6. Write down as many observations as you can.

STRATEGY #3

Before and After Diagrams

Strategy Connections

Thinking Routine: Observe and Wonder

Science Activity: Can You Lift This?, page 67

When to Use: Before the activity
            After the activity

The Before and After Diagram strategy (adapted from Keely, 2008) offers students the opportunity to make their thinking and mental models visible through visuals. The diagrams can be labelled to further enhance explanations and track changes students see occurring in materials used in the activity. By tracking and displaying changes in phenomena, students are better able to identify possible cause-and-effect relationships. Using this strategy provides teachers with more detailed insight into a student's thinking and mental models, and can help identify student misconceptions.

Using the Strategy with the Can You Lift This? Activity

During Science Time

- Start by posing a question that will elicit students' thinking about what is possible during the activity. For example, ask students to consider whether we can pick up a jar of rice with a pencil. Proceed to set up the jar of rice and insert the pencil. Have students draw and label an initial or *Before* diagram of the materials, perhaps using the Before and After strategy organizer on page 65.
- Begin the activity by drawing students' attention to what you are doing (pushing the pencil into the jar) and the effect it is having on the rice in the jar (compacting the grains of rice). Once you have completed the activity, prompt students to draw and label an *After* diagram (using the Before and After strategy organizer on page 65) to capture the changes they see. Encourage students to provide a caption beneath the diagrams to summarize the change(s) they have seen from the Before stage to the After stage. Have students share their Before and After Diagrams with a partner and provide feedback that can be used to revise diagrams.

Variations/Tips/Useful Prompts

- This strategy could be expanded to a Before, During, and After strategy (Keeley, 2008), which would prompt students to capture, in a visual way, what change is happening during the activity as well.
- Online drawing tools and graphics could be useful to students to help them focus on capturing the changes they see in the materials (the level of the rice, the spacing between grains of rice) rather than focusing on drawing container shapes (the jar or bottle that holds the rice).

During Language-Arts Time

- Introduce infographics to students as a different text form they can use to present information and learning in science. Use the Before and After Diagrams: Infographics strategy organizer on page 66 to guide students in understanding what an infographic is and its essential features. Generally, infographics clearly organize information and visuals to tell a story and include

  - distinctive titles, subtitles, and fonts to draw attention to the information being presented

- graphs, charts, statistics, and numbers
- eye-catching visuals
- bold color schemes

- Have several different science-related infographics available for students to examine and deconstruct so they recognize the features listed above. Students can work in pairs to create an infographic that uses their After diagram and to do further research to help them explain the scientific concepts of friction and compaction, and real-life applications of these concepts.

The ABCs of Background Knowledge *Activate, Build, Connect*	Vocabulary Spotlight
Friction: when an object rubs against another, creating resistance to motion • Pencil movement up and down on the rice compacts the rice	*Friction* • From Latin *fricare*, meaning "chafing, rubbing" *Compaction* • Base word *compact* means "to pack or press closely together" • Related words: compact, impact

Before and After Diagrams

Before

Sketch the container holding the rice in the space provided below. Be sure to sketch in rice grains to show how they are spaced and the level they reach in the container.

Caption: _____

_____

After

Sketch the container holding the rice again. Be sure to show any changes you see to its contents.

Caption: _____

_____

Pembroke Publishers ©2023 *Fail-Safe Strategies for Science and Literacy* by Sandra Mirabelli and Lionel Sandner ISBN 978-1-55138-364-4

Before and After Diagrams: Infographics

The term *infographic* is made up of two parts: *info* and *graphic*. Use the word parts to write a definition that explains what an infographic is in the box below.

In·fo·graph·ic (noun) pronounced: /infō'grafik/

Features of Infographics

As you take a look at some example infographics, record some of the features that make them unique.

Use the space below to plan what you might include on an infographic to explain the science behind the Can You Lift This? activity.

Pembroke Publishers ©2023 *Fail-Safe Strategies for Science and Literacy* by Sandra Mirabelli and Lionel Sandner ISBN 978-1-55138-364-4

Can You Lift This?

Fill a narrow rim, long-necked jar with rice. Push a pencil into the jar 20 to 30 times. The pencil will be increasingly hard to push into the jar as the rice packs down. Eventually you will be able to lift the jar with the pencil.

Hints

- As you pack the rice, you might need to add more.
- A glass jar for pouring a liquid like maple syrup works best.

Explanation

The force of pushing the pencil into the jar slowly packs the rice and removes the space between the grains. You will notice it requires more force to push the pencil into the rice. Eventually, the friction between the pencil and the rice will be great enough that you can lift the jar with the pencil.

Supplies

- glass jar with narrow rim and long neck
- rice
- sharpened pencil

Directions

1. Fill the jar with rice.
2. Push the pencil into the rice as far as you can and still be able to pull the pencil out.
3. Repeat 20 to 30 times.
4. When the pencil is firmly lodged in the rice, lift the jar.

Think, Question, Explore

Strategy Connections

Thinking Routine: Observe and Wonder
Science Activity: Candy Color Wheel, page 70
When to Use: Before the activity
              After the activity

Similar to the KWL strategy, the Think, Question, Explore strategy (adapted from Ritchhart, Church & Morrison, 2011) offers students the opportunity to consider what they already know about a topic or phenomenon and to identify areas or questions of interest that could guide further exploration as a result of witnessing what happens in an activity.

Using the Strategy with the Candy Color Wheel Activity

During Science Time

- Have students consider what they **think** they know about the candy M&M's, and what they **think** might happen if it is immersed in water. Students record their thinking on the Think, Question, Explore strategy organizer on page 69.
- After conducting the activity, engage students in a discussion about what they saw happening to the candy and the water. Ask students to use the strategy organizer to record what was surprising or unexpected about the results of the activity and any **questions** they have.
- Encourage students to share their questions and engage in conversations about how they could **explore** them. Provide time for students to research online and share their findings.

Variations/Tips/Useful Prompts

- While students wait for the group activity to show results, have each student fill a 30–60 ml/¼ cup plastic cup to the halfway point with water. Have each student choose one M&M's candy and place it in the cup with the logo facing up. This small-scale, individual activity will help students explore the company's claim that the candy "melts in your mouth, not in your hands."
- Remind students of the other tips and strategies for observing and wondering that the class has been using with various science activities to ensure they are looking closely at the phenomenon that occurs.

During Language-Arts Time

- Before the activity, engage students by showing a video clip of an old M&M's commercial or print ad that features the slogan, "Melts in your mouth, not in your hands!" Ask students to consider whether they believe this slogan to be true, based on their prior experience with the candy. Engage in a discussion about how this slogan (or claim) made by the candy company could be tested. Pairs of students could then write a procedure that would allow them to test this claim during science class.
- Spark further curiosity by having students wonder why the candy doesn't melt in the consumer's hands. Prompt students to explore the ingredient list on the packaging. Which ingredients are familiar? Which are unfamiliar? Provide time for students to think about and research which ingredients could prevent the candy from melting when held in their hands.

The ABCs of Background Knowledge

Activate, Build, Connect

Diffusion: a mixing process in which the particles of one substance spread out in the particles of another substance to create more balance between the two substances
- As the food dye dissolves into water, the color spreads out because of diffusion

---

Vocabulary Spotlight

Diffusion
- From Latin *diffusus* meaning "to spread out"
- Related word: diffuse

Solubility
- From Latin *solu* meaning "to loosen, unfasten"
- Related words: solute, solvent

Think, Question, Explore

What do you **think** you know?

What **questions** do you have about the results of the activity?

How might you **explore** the questions you have?

Candy Color Wheel

In this activity, students place four or five different colored M&M's candies on a paper plate. The plate is filled with enough water to cover the M&M's. After several minutes, the color dye from each candy will diffuse and spread until the colors meet.

Hints

- The plates need to be deep enough to immerse M&M's in water.
- Have extra paper towels available to clean up spills.

Explanation

Once the M&M's candy is covered in water, it begins to dissolve. After the protective wax coating comes off, the colored dye dissolves and begins to spread into the water. This natural motion of the dye particles is called *diffusion*. You can observe the rate of diffusion by watching the color spread out from each of the candies until the colors meet.

Supplies

- paper plates
- enough M&M's candies for each group to have 4 or 5 different-colored candies
- water (approximately 250 ml/1 cup)

Directions

1. Place M&M's equally spaced on the plate.
2. Slowly add water until candies are submerged.
3. Record observations over a period of about ten minutes.

Q-Chart Question Prompts

Strategy Connections

Thinking Routine: Observe and Wonder
Science Activity: Kissing Candles, page 73
When to Use: After the activity

When asked to create questions, students readily generate *what, when,* and *where* questions, but creating higher-order *how might* and *why would* questions does not come as naturally to them. The Q-Chart Question Prompts strategy helps students generate a large volume and variety of questions that are of personal interest. Modelling and encouraging students to use the question-creation chart, or Q-chart, provides a framework that ensures questions range from close-ended, factual questions to more open-ended, divergent-thinking questions.

Using the Strategy with the Kissing Candles Activity

During Science Time

After students have observed the candle re-light, have them consider what questions they might have about this phenomenon. Using the My Q-Chart Questions strategy organizer on page 72, guide students to select one word from the left side of the Q-chart (*Who, What, When, Where, How, Why*) and pair it with a word along the top of the chart (*is, did, can, would, will, might*). Using these two words as a question starter, students write the question they develop in the box where the two words intersect on the organizer. Encourage them to choose two new words and write new questions related to the activity on the Q-chart.

Variations/Tips/Useful Prompts

- Using the Q-chart strategy will assist students in moving beyond their *why* questions to deeper-level questioning. By combining "how" with "might" or "will," for example, students can generate a multitude of questions that are testable.
- Encourage students to consider the materials that were used and what you did when demonstrating the activity. For example, students might focus on the type of candle used, the size of the candles (length or thickness), the distance between the candles, or even the length of time before the blown-out candle is placed back into the convection current. Questions, such as *How might changing the type of candle used affect whether the candle re-lights?* or *How will increasing the distance between the lit candles affect whether the blown-out candle re-lights?,* can lead to a class discussion on manipulating variables in science.

The ABCs of Background Knowledge

Activate, Build, Connect

Convection Current: The cycle created when heated fluid molecules rise and then sink as they cool

- Air is the fluid that rises from the heat of the candle flame. Cooler air rushes in from below the flame to create the convection current.

Vocabulary Spotlight

Convection
- Root word *convect* means "to carry (heat or air)"
- Related words: heat, thermal energy transfer

Combustion
- From Latin *comburere,* meaning "to burn"

During Language-Arts Time

- Engage students in a discussion about the importance of wondering and asking questions in science. You might want to create a class anchor chart about what wondering/asking questions looks like, sounds like, and feels like.
- Share or revisit the two quotes at the bottom of the My Q-Chart Questions strategy organizer on page 72 and comment on how many people from a variety of fields have reflected on the value of asking good questions. Provide students with some time to research other famous quotes about the importance of questions and asking questions in science. Students can contribute their quote and explain what it means to them in a shared class space, such as a slide deck.

My Q-Chart Questions

	is	did	can	would	will	might
Who						
What						
When						
Where						
How						
Why						

"A scientist is not a person who gives the right answers, but one who asks the right questions."
— C. Levi-Strauss

"If I had an hour to solve a problem and my life depended on the solution, I would spend the first 55 minutes determining the proper question to ask… "
— Albert Einstein

Pembroke Publishers ©2023 *Fail-Safe Strategies for Science and Literacy* by Sandra Mirabelli and Lionel Sandner ISBN 978-1-55138-364-4

Kissing Candles

In this activity, you light two candles and place one flame directly under the other, then remove the bottom candle so it is positioned away from the other and blow out the flame from the candle you moved. When you immediately place the candle back into its initial position, you can observe the candle being re-lit.

Hints

- Non-drip candles make less of a mess.
- Place a tray below the candles to catch melted wax.
- Follow all safety procedures related to using an open flame.

Explanation

Candles burn because of the chemical reaction of combustion. For combustion to occur, there must be fuel, oxygen, and an ignition source. When the two candles are lined up, one above the other, a convection current forms. As the heated air around the candle rises, cooler air is pulled from the bottom. When the blown-out candle is placed back under the lit candle, convection currents move air across the warm wick. The rising smoke particles provide the fuel. The upper candle flame is the ignition source. Now combustion can re-occur because there is fuel, oxygen, and an ignition source. The candle re-lights.

Supplies

- 2 candles
- lighter
- tray
- safety equipment as needed

Directions

1. Light two candles.
2. Place one candle flame about 5 cm/2 inches below the other.
3. Remove the bottom candle and blow it out.
4. Quickly move the candle back to its original position.
5. Observe the bottom candle re-lighting.

Safety

Follow your school board's safety policy related to open flame in the classroom.

Inference Ladder

Strategy Connections
Thinking Routine: Predict and Infer
Science Activity: Inference Cube, page 76
When to Use: During the activity
After the activity

The Inference Ladder strategy (adapted from Senge, 2006) helps students slow down their thinking so that they better use available data/observations to make informed inferences. Purposeful stops on the different rungs of the ladder going up will lead students to select and interpret observations so that they may come to logical conclusions.

Using the Strategy with the Inference Cube Activity

- While doing the Inference Cube science activity, have students record as many observations as they can about the five sides of the cube that are visible to them in the Observation box at the bottom of the Ladder of Inference strategy organizer on page 75. For example, students might observe that names on the cube are written in different colors, some names appear in purple ink, or there is a number in the top left corner on each side. Discard any duplicate observations.
- As they work in their groups, encourage students to consider and group similar observations in separate boxes as they go up the ladder on the strategy organizer. For example, all the observations about the names can be grouped together in one box and observations about the number in the bottom left corner can be grouped in another box. Prompt them to record the grouping rule they used above each list of observations.
- Finally, have students infer and write what they believe would appear (name and numbers) on the bottom of the inference cube, which is not visible to them, in the box at the top of the inference ladder. Remind them that this decision should be based on the conclusions they have drawn from their observations and inferences further down the ladder.

Variations/Tips/Useful Prompts
- To stimulate thinking, it might be useful to embed pause-and-share points during the group-work time. Each group can offer one thing they noticed or observed about the cube without expanding to the conclusions they draw from that observation.
- Encourage students to quietly call you over when they think they know what would appear at the bottom of the cube. This will allow all groups to continue solving the mystery.
- There are many other variations of inference cubes available online; alternatively, you can challenge students to create one of their own for the class to try.

The ABCs of Background Knowledge

Activate, Build, Connect

Model/Black Box: a physical or visual representation of an idea, process, or system that helps describe phenomena in the natural world that we can't experience directly
- By collecting evidence of patterns, we can infer what is on the side that we can't see

---

Vocabulary Spotlight

Scientific Law: a description of what always happens, based on observations and results of experiments; e.g., Newton's Laws of Motion
Scientific Theory: an explanation of why things happen, based on observations and results of experiments; e.g., the theory of gravity
- Related words: theoretical, theory

The Ladder of Inference

STEP 3
Draw Conclusions
What is on the bottom of the cube?

STEP 2

Sort observations

OBSERVATIONS	OBSERVATIONS	OBSERVATIONS

STEP 1

Record all of your group observations

- There is a name on each side in the middle

Pembroke Publishers ©2023 *Fail-Safe Strategies for Science and Literacy* by Sandra Mirabelli and Lionel Sandner ISBN 978-1-55138-364-4

Inference Cube

The inference cube has five sides with a name and numbers in colors on each of five sides; each side is connected to the side opposite it in a pattern. The sixth side of the cube, facing downwards, is blank. By observing the patterns on the five visible sides, you can infer the word and numbers on the hidden/blank side.

Hint

- There are two big ideas in this activity:

    1. Patterns can be determined, inferred from evidence that is collected.
    2. Models can be inferred and created, based on the evidence collected to explain natural phenomena we can't observe directly.

Explanation

The inference cube pictured in the margin has the following patterns:

X_1 – top right corner: number of letters in name on opposite side
X_2 – bottom left corner: number of letters both names have in common
X_3 – name: commonly female on one side, commonly male on the opposite side
X_4 – colors: same as opposite side

Directions

1. Place cube on table, blank side down
2. Determine what should be written on the side of the cube you can't observe.

Think, Pair, Share, Draw

The seemingly simple Think, Pair, Share strategy provides students with time to first think on their own about their response to a prompt or question, which results in better quality responses. Pairing and sharing their thinking with another student provides an opportunity for students to hear and consider differing perspectives and ideas. By interacting with a peer, students can gain new knowledge or refine their own thinking. This peer interaction also builds student confidence in sharing their ideas in a larger class discussion after obtaining feedback. For the Think, Pair, Share, Draw strategy, we add one more step by having students create a drawing to help them explain what they believe to be happening.

Using the Strategy with the Inference Can Activity

- Choose a point during the activity where it would be beneficial for students to stop and think about what is happening. For example, in the Inference Can activity on page 79, it is important for students to have an opportunity to experience several variations of what happens when one of the strings protruding from the side of the can is pulled *before* starting to use the strategy.
- Prompt students to **think** to themselves about what the interior construction of the can might look like. Have them consider what they have observed about the behavior of the strings on the outside of the can when one is pulled to infer how the string(s) might be arranged inside the can. Ask students to **pair** with a table partner and **share** their ideas. They can **draw** a diagram of the string arrangement inside the can using the Think, Pair, Share, Draw strategy organizer on page 78. Engage the class in discussion, allowing for the sharing of some diagrams, so that students can consider how confident they are in their model and any refining they might want to do before creating their own inference can.

Variations/Tips/Useful Prompts

- There are a number of common variations to this strategy, including Think, Pair, Share, Square, in which two pairs join together for a second round of sharing. In science it can be helpful to add the Draw phase, and even a Do phase, to this strategy, so that students are engaged in the activity and in other ways of representing their thinking before or after sharing (adapted from P. Keeley, 2008).
- In larger group discussions, following the Share phase of this strategy, students can share, with the whole group, their own ideas or parts of the conversation they had in the pairing. Be sure to emphasize that it is important that they verbally acknowledge when they are sharing their partner's good ideas.

The ABCs of Background Knowledge

Activate, Build, Connect

Inference: a conclusion you make based on evidence and background knowledge
- The skill of inferring is used across the curriculum, especially in science and language arts, to think beyond a text or about an object or event in the natural world.

Vocabulary Spotlight

Inference
- Root word *infer* means "to conclude or deduce"
- Related words: infer, inferential, inferior

Think, Pair, Share, Draw with the Inference Can

I THINK the interior of the can looks like this

because…

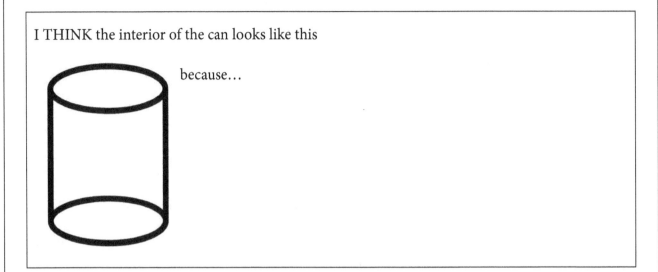

MY PARTNER THINKS the interior of the can looks like this

because…

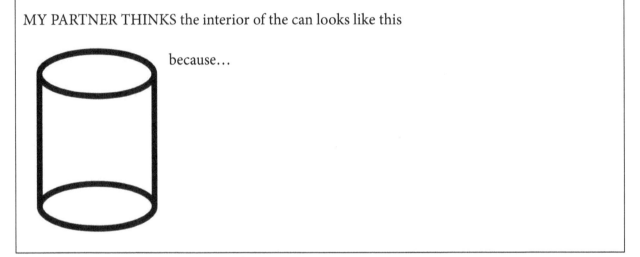

WE decided the interior of the can we construct will look like this

because…

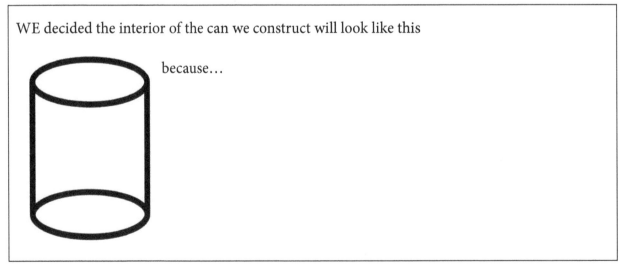

Pembroke Publishers ©2023 *Fail-Safe Strategies for Science and Literacy* by Sandra Mirabelli and Lionel Sandner ISBN 978-1-55138-364-4

Inference Can

Four strands of rope are hanging out of four holes in a potato chip can. Pull on each string separately and something different happens to the other three strings. The task is to infer how the strings are arranged inside the sealed can.

Hint

- Make sure the cans are sealed so no one can peek inside to see the answer.

Explanation

The diagram to the left shows how the strings should be arranged in the can. Each string is about 40 cm/16 inches long.

Supplies

For each inference can, use:
- 2 pieces of rope, each 40 cm/16 inches long
- 1 empty potato chip can

Preparation

1. Make two holes on opposite sides of the can about a quarter of the way down from the top.
2. Make a second set of two holes on opposite sides of the can about a quarter of the way up from the bottom.
3. Thread one string through the top two holes, leaving plenty of slack.
4. Thread the second string through one of the bottom holes and then over the first string and back through the second hole.
5. Adjust strings so that equal lengths hang out of the can.

Directions

1. Pull on each of the strings and observe the results.
2. Using the Think, Pair, Share, Draw with the Inference Can organizer, infer how the strings are arranged inside the can.

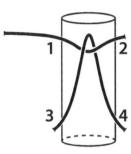

Diagram by Owen Sandner

STRATEGY #8
Trending Now

Strategy Connections

Thinking Routine: Predict and Infer
Science Activity: Geyser in a Bottle, page 84
When to Use: Before the activity
After the activity

Social media posts can be drafted but might not be shared online.

The Trending Now strategy encourages students to synthesize ideas to create a captivating social media post about an activity they will participate in. Students consider the scientific phenomenon before it occurs and add their own creative use of language to write in the style of a social media post that will entice readers to want to know more about the phenomenon. Creating an intriguing headline and expanding it into a social media post or short news item will allow students to demonstrate their skill in predicting the outcome of the activity.

Using the Strategy with the Geyser in a Bottle Activity

During Science Time

- Have students consider the materials you will provide for the Geyser in a Bottle activity on page 84. Prompt students to predict what they think will happen when they drop Mentos™ candies into the bottle of soda. Working in their groups, students can use the Trending Now strategy organizer on page 82 to consider possible outcomes of this activity and then to develop a short, catchy headline to entice others to watch what happens. Encourage students to use descriptive language in their headline to capture the readers' attention and build anticipation. Their headline, a prediction of what students expect to happen, will be confirmed or refuted as the class does the activity.
- After the activity is completed, students can return to the Trending Now organizer to reflect on what happened and indicate whether their prediction was confirmed. They can then write a revised headline that will capture readers' attention and build anticipation, as well as record several important things they learned in this activity. Now students can draft a short social media post about the activity and consider a visual they would add to this post.

Variations/Tips/Useful Prompts

- Some students will be familiar with this activity from popular media. Encourage students to think about descriptive words they can use as part of their headline to either describe the action they anticipate or to relate this action to a real world phenomenon that would behave in the same way; for example, a fountain, geyser, or volcano.
- Expand on this strategy after the activity to have students communicate their understanding of the reaction that took place when combining the soda and Mentos™ candies. Continuing with the Trending Now strategy at the end of the activity will engage students in synthesizing their experience of the activity with the class discussion of why this happened, to produce writing that explains the essence of the activity and the science behind it.

During Language-Arts Time

- Have students look at online newspapers and social media forums with a focus on collecting headlines that catch their attention and draw them into reading more of the accompanying article or post. Prompt students to share the headlines they find engaging with the rest of the class through conversation or via a digital or other platform. Discuss why certain titles captured their attention. For example, it might be helpful to share with students that headlines or titles of news items often

- use just a few words or a phrase to capture the main idea or essence of a topic or event
- play on words by using a well-known phrase or word related to the topic/event in a different way
- provide enough detail to entice someone to want to know more

- Have students return to the social media post they created for the Geyser in a Bottle activity on page 84 in science class and see if they can improve their Trending Now headline and social media post. Can they use some of the characteristics discussed in language class to write a new and more enticing post?
- Alternatively, students can consider the news headlines provided on the Trending Now: Headlines strategy organizer on page 83, and identify which ones are most enticing and why. Use this activity to help students deconstruct the characteristics of good headlines as identified above, then prompt them to return to their attempt in science to write a headline and post for the science activity.

The ABCs of Background Knowledge *Activate, Build, Connect*	Vocabulary Spotlight
Physical Change: a change in size, shape, appearance, state of matter; the substance does not become a different substance • The carbon dioxide in the diet soda phase changes to a gas when it comes in contact with the candy. This physical change happens rapidly and creates a fountain effect.	*Geyser* • From Icelandic *geysir* meaning "to gush" • Synonyms: jet, spring, fountain

Trending Now

Before the Activity

Predict some of the possible outcomes of this activity in the box below.

Write a headline for a social media post based on what you think will happen in the activity.

After the Activity

Was your prediction confirmed? Refuted? Explain.

List some of the important things you learned as a result of this activity. (It might be helpful to think about the following: carbon dioxide, pressure, bubbles.)

Rewrite your headline here, along with a short social media post or news report about what happened in the activity and explaining the science behind it.

Pembroke Publishers ©2023 *Fail-Safe Strategies for Science and Literacy* by Sandra Mirabelli and Lionel Sandner ISBN 978-1-55138-364-4

Trending Now: Headlines

The Straw that Broke the Camel's Back: It's Plastic!
Queen Goes Green: Bans Drinking Straws from her Palaces
Restaurants Find Plastic Straw Alternatives
The Last Straw: Should this Plastic Relic Go?
Anti-straw Movement Chokes on New Bill
Dermatologists Warn Against Danger of Straws

Which of the headlines captured your interest and would make you read more of the social media post about banning plastic straws? Write those headlines in the box below.

Writers can use a lot of different techniques to capture a reader's attention. How have you decided on a title for some of the writing you have done? Explain your thinking and/or your process.

Thinking Like a Writer

What is it about the headlines above that makes them interesting? Choose 1 or 2 of the headlines to explain your point(s).

Pembroke Publishers ©2023 *Fail-Safe Strategies for Science and Literacy* by Sandra Mirabelli and Lionel Sandner ISBN 978-1-55138-364-4

I first wrote about this activity in the late 1990s before it became a YouTube sensation. While it's been performed in almost every way possible, it's still a great example of a physical change.

Safety

Keep a safe distance from the bottle once the candy has been dropped into it.

Geyser in a Bottle

Summary

Drop a Mentos™ candy into soda pop and watch the release of carbon dioxide create a large volume of foam. The extra surface area from the candy causes the carbon dioxide from the soda to rapidly come out of solution.

Hints

- Use diet soda, as the liquid is not as sticky and is easier to clean up.
- Try different types of candy and observe the effect.

Explanation

There appears to be a variety of possible explanations for the cause of the foam production, but the simplest appears to be the carbon dioxide gas in the soda comes out of solution when the candy is added to the soda. The bumpy surface found on the candy creates the ideal conditions for the carbon dioxide to change state from liquid to gas.

Supplies

- package of Mentos™ candy
- 2L bottle of diet soda

Directions

1. Place a large, plastic 2L bottle of soda in a large pan, preferably in a location that is easy to clean up.
2. Remove lid from soda bottle.
3. Carefully drop one candy into the bottle.
4. Quickly step back and observe.

Predict, Explain, Observe, Explain (PEOE)

The Predict, Explain, Observe, Explain—or PEOE—strategy (adapted from White & Gunstone, 1992) engages students in inquiry during a demonstration or activity by prompting them to predict what they think will happen, based on prior knowledge. The strategy also prompts students to think deeply in order to explain their prediction before observing the activity and to explain what did happen. Using this strategy makes students' thinking visible and can help teachers identify misconceptions, as students gather and interpret data during the activity to draw evidence-based conclusions.

Using the Strategy with the Piercing Pencils Activity

During Science Time

- Start by having students **predict** what they think will happen in the Piercing Pencils activity on page 88. Students can record their prediction in Box 1 on the PEOE strategy organizer on page 87.
- In Box 2, students **explain** how they know their prediction is likely, using their prior experience and reasoning skills to guide them.
- While the activity is conducted, students can record **observations** in Box 3 on the strategy organizer. For example, they might write, *3 pencils were pushed through the bag of water, the bag of water is ¾ of the way full and the bag of water is sealed at the top.* Encourage students to include a labelled diagram as well.
- Box 4 prompts students to re-evaluate their **prediction**, based on their observations from the actual activity, and to revise their **explanation**, based on these observations and the class discussion during the activity.

Variations/Tips/Useful Prompts

- It could be helpful to frame the activity at the start with a guiding question; for example, *What will happen when I push a sharp pencil through a bag full of water?* This will support students in making their predictions.
- If supporting information on polymers, in the form of an online article or textbook entry, is available, it can be shared to help students expand their second explanation in the PEOE strategy and to supplement the class discussion.
- Providing key words, like *polymers*, for students to incorporate in their final Explain, reminds students to incorporate scientific terminology and understanding in the final part of the strategy.
- Doubling the final *E* in the strategy to add Extend would prompt students to apply what they have learned to the real world and to think about how their new knowledge might present some solutions to real-life problems.

During Language-Arts Time

- Use the PEOE strategy to frame conversations about texts you are reading together. Modelling the use of the strategy will build familiarity for future use during science time. The Predict/Explain phase could be based on the cover of a picture book or the events in a short story. For the Observe/Explain phase of the strategy, you could use two pause points. For the first, pause partway through the text and have students revisit and possibly revise their predictions once they have gathered more information in the text or story. This will support students in analyzing their thinking and in realizing that, with more information, we can make better predictions and our thinking may change. A second pause point in the Observe/Explain phase would occur at the end of the text, where students can reflect on whether their prediction was affirmed or refuted.

- Language arts time also offers the opportunity for the class to discuss and distinguish between making a prediction in science and making a prediction in language arts. In language arts we tend to use the formula

  evidence in the text + your background knowledge = an inference

  This formula describes a special type of inference that is future-focused. In science the same formula can be used; however, it is important to emphasize that the background knowledge students are using is their scientific background knowledge, and that evidence is collected from observations.

- Consider selecting and reading texts about plastics, how they are made, and the environmental issues we face as a result of their use, or texts that explain what polymers are and their characteristics. In this way, you can help build students' background knowledge related to this science activity.

The ABCs of Background Knowledge *Activate, Build, Connect*	Vocabulary Spotlight
Plastic: human-made material composed of polymers or long repeating chains of molecules • The pencil pushes the polymer strands apart and creates space for it to penetrate the plastic bag.	*Polymer* • Root *mer* meaning "part or segment" • Prefix *poly* meaning "many" • Related words: polyurethane, polyester

PEOE: Predict, Explain, Observe, Explain

What will happen when I push a sharp pencil through a bag full of water?

1. Predict → What do you think will happen? Include a labelled diagram to help show your prediction.	**2. Explain** ↓ Why do you think this will happen? Do you have any scientific background knowledge that helps you explain your prediction?
4. Explain Do your observations support your initial prediction? What have you learned in this activity?	← **3. Observe** What happened? Record your observations.

Pembroke Publishers ©2023 *Fail-Safe Strategies for Science and Literacy* by Sandra Mirabelli and Lionel Sandner ISBN 978-1-55138-364-4

Piercing Pencils

Summary

Fill a resealable bag with water. Take a sharp pencil and carefully push the tip into the plastic bag. Keep pushing until the pencil tip comes out the other side.

Hints

- Ensure the pencil tip is sharp.
- When pushing the pencil through the bag, make sure to make one slow, smooth push, rather than stopping and starting.

Explanation

Plastic is made up of long, fibre-like chains of polymers that overlap each other. This gives plastic properties of being flexible, waterproof, and stretchy. When you push the sharp pencil tip through the plastic, you are pushing the long fibres out of the way. The resulting hole does not change the properties of the plastic and the integrity of the plastic bag is not damaged. The resulting pencil or pencils through the bag create a great effect without spilling water.

Supplies

- 4–6 sharpened pencils
- plastic resealable bag
- water

Directions

1. Sharpen your pencils.
2. Fill a resealable bag three-quarters full of water and seal the bag.
3. Slowly and firmly push a pencil through the bag until the pencil comes out the other side.
4. Repeat until all your pencils are inserted through the bag of water.

Poll Everyone

Strategy Connections

Thinking Routine: Predict and Infer
Science Activity: Egg in a Cup, page 92
When to Use: Before the activity

The Poll Everyone strategy engages students in predicting the outcome of an activity, based on related background knowledge and experiences they might have with the phenomenon or materials in the activity. Connecting to their background knowledge and experiences will support students in making a prediction, rather than a wild guess, about what could possibly happen in an activity. Making predictions enhances students' attention, as they are now invested in finding out if they were right about the outcome of the activity.

Using the Strategy with the Egg in a Cup Activity

During Science Time

- Have students consider the structure you have built to support the egg in this activity. Remind students that in our own lives, on a daily basis, there are many forces that act on structures. Invite students to identify some of these forces. Students might offer various forces as examples: *the wind, the rain, the weight of people using the structure*, or *the weight of materials used to build the structure*.
- Pose the question, *What will happen to the egg sitting at the top of this structure if I apply a force along the edge of the cookie sheet?*
- Prompt students to predict what they think will happen to the egg. Working individually and then in pairs, students can use the Precariously Balanced strategy organizer on page 91 to consider and record several possible outcomes. Encourage students to use their scientific knowledge of structures and the forces acting on structures, as well as their own ideas, to generate and explain their predictions.
- Have students share their predictions with the class and identify the three or four predictions that come up most often:

    the egg will fall off the structure onto the ground
    the egg will fly forward
    the egg will fly backward onto the person applying the force
    the egg will fall into the cup

- Using an electronic polling tool, provide students with time to enter which choice they feel is most probable. Share the results of the poll with the class and continue with the activity.

Variations/Tips/Useful Prompts

- Polling of students can be done in ways other than electronically. Once the three or four most obvious outcomes are identified, students could raise their hands to predict which outcome they think is most likely. Alternatively, each student could be provided with a small sticky note to post on a chart that identifies the possible outcomes. In this way, you would create a bar graph of possibilities that remains visible to everyone as the activity continues.
- Consider having students revisit their initial predictions and discuss how the outcome of the activity makes them reconsider what they think they knew.

- Look for opportunities to revisit predictions part way through the process and have students revise their predictions, based on new information they have obtained.

During Language-Arts Time

- Students can practice making predictions in language arts using a variety of different types of texts, including written, visual, and media texts.
- It is important to help students see that there is a key difference when making predictions in language arts from making them in science. In language arts, we make predictions based on our background knowledge and evidence in the text we are reading or viewing. In science, that background knowledge needs to be scientific background knowledge. This is where language-arts time spent reading and making sense of informational texts related to phenomena and concepts currently being studied in science can help build and broaden background knowledge. To support the Egg in a Cup activity, you might consider texts that build knowledge about structures and the forces that act on them; for example, there might be recent news articles or video clips of weather events related to these concepts that highlight a phenomenon, such as a hurricane or tornado, and its effect on buildings.

The ABCs of Background Knowledge *Activate, Build, Connect*	Vocabulary Spotlight
Newton's First Law of Motion: an object will stay at rest or in motion until some outside force starts it moving, speeds it up, slows it down, or changes its direction of movement. • The egg's inertia keeps it in place, so that it does not move until a force removes the cookie sheet and spool of thread from underneath it. Then gravity acts on the egg to overcome its inertia, and the egg falls in the cup.	*Exert* • Root *ert* meaning "to push out, to put forth" • Prefix *ex–* meaning "out of, from" (Sometimes, the prefix *ex–* means "not, without.") • Related word: exertion • Synonyms: apply, wield, exercise

Precariously Balanced

Activating My Related Background Knowledge

What do you know about the stability of structures and about the forces acting on structures that might help you predict what will happen in this activity?

Working with a partner, use the boxes below to predict some of the possible outcomes of this activity. For each of your predictions, explain why you think this might happen.

My Prediction

My Partner's Prediction

Egg in a Cup

Summary

Place an egg on top of a structure built of a coffee mug filled halfway with water, with a cookie sheet on top of the cup and a spool of thread placed directly above with the cup and on top of the cookie sheet. Position the structure so the cookie sheet is just poking over the edge of a table. Firmly place your foot on the end of a straw broom and pull back the handle. When you release the broom handle, it should just hit the cookie sheet before hitting the edge of the table. Watch what happens to the egg!

Hints

- Start with a cup that has a large circumference at the top.
- Use a straw broom with a wooden handle.
- Make sure the egg is in line with the cup.
- The cookie sheet must have a smooth bottom, so it slides off the top of the cup.

Explanation

When the broom handle hits the cookie sheet, a force is applied that causes the sheet to slide off the cup. The friction between the spool of thread and cookie sheet pulls the spool along with the cookie sheet. There is less friction between the egg and the spool, so the egg is not pulled along. Now the only force acting on the egg is gravity, so it falls into the cup.

Supplies

- coffee cup
- cookie sheet
- spool of thread
- egg (raw)
- straw broom
- half cup of water

Directions

1. Place the coffee cup half full of water on a table.
2. Balance the cookie sheet on the cup.
3. Place the spool of thread on top of the cookie sheet so that spool is directly above the coffee cup.
4. Carefully balance the egg on the spool of thread.
5. Position the straw broom so your foot holds the broom end down and the handle can be pulled back, allowing it to hit the cookie sheet just before it hits the table. This will take a bit of repositioning of the cup/sheet/spool/egg structure.
6. Pull back on the broom handle and release in one firm, swift motion.
7. Watch the egg fall into the cup. And everyone claps!

Question Sorter

Strategy Connections
Thinking Routine: Sort and Classify
Science Activity: Crushed Can, page 97
When to Use: After the activity

Involving students in questioning in the science classroom promotes engagement and curiosity. The Question Sorter strategy encourages students to consider three types of questions they might encounter in science: testable, researchable, and ponderable questions. By considering these question types, students gain insight into what is involved in answering their question(s) and to what extent their question(s) can actually be answered.

Using the Strategy with the Crushed Can Activity

During Science Time

After the activity, allow time for students to generate questions related to the crushed can. Encourage students to record one question on each of the sticky notes or cue cards they are provided. Students can then work in pairs to consider what types of questions they have generated—using the categories *testable*, *researchable*, and *ponderable*—and to sort them into the corresponding areas on the Question Sorter strategy organizer on page 95. Provide time for students to share their questions and discuss what could be done to answer some of them.

Variations/Tips/Useful Prompts

- In language arts, students might have used the Question–Answer Relationship (QAR) strategy (see below) when reading a text to consider the four places they could find answers to their questions (*right there, think and search, the author and me*, or *on my own*). The Question Sorter strategy is specifically designed for science to help students consider the question–answer relationship from a scientific context.
- When sorting questions, students consider whether each question is

    Testable: Is this a question that we would investigate through another science activity to answer it? Questions of this type might include *What would happen if we use a larger can? Would the can collapse if the water in the pan was at room temperature?*

    Researchable: Is this a question we could find an answer for by doing some research online, in a textbook, or by using other texts available to us? For example: *What caused the aluminum can to collapse?*

    Ponderable: Is this a question for which more information could be obtained if we conducted an investigation or did some research, but that, ultimately, will not have a definitive answer?

During Language-Arts Time

- Have students review their researchable and ponderable questions to consider sources (online or in the classroom) that might provide answers to their questions. Discuss, as a class, whether they would expect to find answers to their questions explicitly in a text or would have to make connections and infer across several texts, as well as use what they already know about the topic of air pressure and how it might relate to the crushed can activity or another activity you have engaged in.

- Introduce or review the Question–Answer Relationship (QAR) strategy (you can use the Question–Answer Relationship strategy organizer on page 96) with students by reminding them that there is a relationship between the questions we have and where to find answers. Categorizing the types of questions we have helps us determine if the answer will be found on the pages in the text or if we will need to infer or read between or beyond the lines to find an answer.

- There are 4 types of relationships to consider:

   Right There: The answer is explicitly stated in the text .

   Here and There: The answer is found by combining pieces of information from different parts of the text.

   The Author and Me: Students will need to combine clues or evidence in the text with their own prior scientific knowledge to answer the question.

   On My Own: Students will need to think about the topic, their prior scientific knowledge, and what they've read now or previously to make connections and answer the question.

Students can use the Question-Answer Relationship strategy organizer on page 96.

Provide time for students to carry out the research needed to answer some of their questions and report back to the class on their findings.

The ABCs of Background Knowledge *Activate, Build, Connect*	Vocabulary Spotlight
Pressure: the amount of force exerted on an area • Boiling water in the can and flipping it over into ice water lowers the pressure inside the can, causing the atmospheric pressure to implode the can.	*Temperature* • From Latin *temperatura* meaning "degree of heat or cold" • Related word: temperate *Atmospheric* • From *Greek* atmos meaning "steam or vapor"; *spheric* meaning "sphere or globe" *Implosion* • From Latin meaning "a sudden collapse inward"; modelled on *explosion*; prefix *in–* meaning "into, in" • Related words: implode • Synonym: collapse • Antonym: explode, explosion

Question Sorter

Testable Questions

Would any of your questions require us to set up an investigation or experiment and gather the results to answer it? Place those questions in this box.

Researchable Questions

Could we find an answer to your question(s) by researching online, looking in a textbook, or using other texts available to us? Place those questions in this box.

Ponderable Questions

Do your questions seem significant and important, but you are unsure whether we can come up with a definite answer, either through further investigation or research? Place those questions this box.

Pembroke Publishers ©2023 *Fail-Safe Strategies for Science and Literacy* by Sandra Mirabelli and Lionel Sandner ISBN 978-1-55138-364-4

Question–Answer Relationship

My Researchable and Ponderable Questions

Place your questions from above in the appropriate box, based on where you expect to find the answer.

I think I can find the answers…

In text:	In my head:
Right There I will find the answer in one place in the text.	**The Author and Me** I'll make an inference by combining clues the author gives me in the text with what I already know about the topic.
Here and There I will find the answer in several places in the text.	**On My Own** I'll use my related prior knowledge and experience of the topic and my own ideas to answer the question.

Choose 1 or 2 questions from the chart and try to answer them using the strategies for each type.

Pembroke Publishers ©2023 *Fail-Safe Strategies for Science and Literacy* by Sandra Mirabelli and Lionel Sandner ISBN 978-1-55138-364-4

Crushed Can

Summary

On a hotplate, bring an aluminum pop can with about 30 ml/2 tablespoons of water in it to a boil. While waiting, fill a pie plate three quarters full with water and add about a tray of ice cubes. When the water is boiling, carefully use tongs to grab the pop can. Quickly invert and place the can into the ice water. Observe the can being crushed. It happens very fast.

Hints

- Use only a small volume of water in the pop can.
- When placing the can into the cold water, make sure the inverted top surface of the can is parallel to the water. You want the whole surface of the can to hit the water at the same time.
- When placing the can in the cold water, make sure it doesn't hit any ice cubes.

Explanation

Boiling the water creates steam in the can. Inverting the can into the ice water rapidly changes the temperature and condenses the steam. This causes the pressure inside the can to decrease. The atmospheric (outside) pressure then crushes the can.

Supplies

- aluminum pop can
- pie plate
- water
- 1 tray ice cubes
- tongs
- oven mitts
- hot plate

Directions

1. Place 30 ml/2 tablespoons of water into an empty aluminum pop can.
2. Place the pop can on hot plate.
3. Before the water boils, fill the pie plate three quarters full of water and ice.
4. When steam is rising from the pop can, use tongs to carefully grab the pop can.
5. Quickly invert the can as you place it into the water.
6. Observe the pop can.

Safety

Follow your school board's safety policy related to use of hot plates in the classroom.

Chain Notes

Strategy Connections

Thinking Routine: Sort and Classify
Science Activity: Cheese String
Candle, page 100
When to Use: After the activity

The Chain Notes strategy (Keeley, 2008) motivates students to move beyond obvious statements of fact as they review what students before them have already contributed to the "chain" of notes. Once students have considered what has already been said in the class chain note, they can add a new idea, a fact, an example, or an analogy, or build on an idea already stated with a new connection. This is an opportunity for the teacher to check for understanding and depth of thinking, as well as to identify any misconceptions in students' thinking.

Using the Strategy with the Cheese String Candle Activity

During Science Time

- To prepare for this strategy, write an open-ended question or prompt at the top of a paper to be passed around the classroom after the activity is completed. For example, in the Cheese String Candle activity on page 100, you might ask, *How can we distinguish between an observation and an inference?* Alternatively you could prompt students to complete a sentence starter; e.g. *An observation I/we made is…* or *An inference I/we made is…*
- Allow students to pass the note around the classroom, ensuring all students have an opportunity to contribute one or two short sentences to the note. Entries can remain anonymous.

Variations/Tips/Useful Prompts

- This strategy could be done while students are working on another task to make the best use of wait times as the chain note is passed around the classroom.
- The Chain Notes strategy can be used at the start of a topic or lesson to assess the prior knowledge students bring to a given topic or concept. After reviewing the notes, a class discussion could help synthesize ideas and address any misconceptions that are evident in the chain note.
- Alternatively, groups of students can work with copies of the class set of notes to discuss what they agree or disagree with and provide their reasoning.

During Language-Arts Time

Once all students have contributed to the chain note, each group of students could be given a copy of the notes and prompted to sort and organize the chain notes into categories, based on the initial question posed to the class or on other similarities they see in the items in the note. Provide time for each group to present their categories to the class and share what the class has learned as a result of engaging in the Cheese String Candle science activity on page 100.

The ABCs of Background Knowledge
Activate, Build, Connect
Observing: looking closely to describe an object, situation, or event. (See anchor chart on page 30.)   • Observations of the cheese stick candle might cause students to incorrectly infer the composition of the candle.

Vocabulary Spotlight
Observation   • From Latin *observare* meaning " to attend to, to watch over, to look at"   • Related words: observe, observatory

Chain Notes Prompts

Use one of the following prompts to contribute a note:

- *How can we distinguish between an observation and an inference?*
- *An observation I/we made is…*
- *An inference I/we made is…*

Student 1	
Student 2	
Student 3	
Student 4	
Student 5	
Student 6	
Student 7	
Student 8	
Student 9	
Student 10	
Student 11	
Student 12	
Student 13	
Student 14	
Student 15	

Pembroke Publishers ©2023 *Fail-Safe Strategies for Science and Literacy* by Sandra Mirabelli and Lionel Sandner ISBN 978-1-55138-364-4

Cheese Stick Candle

Summary

A simulated candle is created from a mozzarella cheese stick and an almond sliver. Turn the lights down and light the almond sliver. Have students make observations. Blow the candle out and eat the candle for added effect!

Hint

- Be aware of any nut allergies.

Explanation

This activity is designed to help students understand the difference between an observation and an inference. A student comment that relates to the cheese stick being a candle is based on an inference.

Supplies

- mozzarella cheese stick (white cheese looks more like candle wax)
- almond sliver
- lighter

Safety

Follow your school board's safety policy related to use of open flame in the classroom.

Preparation

1. Press the almond sliver into top of the cheese stick.
2. Hold the cheese stick candle so it doesn't flop over.
3. Light the almond sliver with your back turned to class.
4. Turn around and ask for student observations and inferences.

Directions

1. Look at the lit object and make observations and inferences.

STRATEGY #13
List–Group–Label

Strategy Connections

Thinking Routine: Sort and Classify
Science Activity: Reaction in a Bag, page 103
When to Use: Before the activity
          After the activity

The List–Group–Label strategy encourages students to use their critical thinking skills to work with vocabulary related to a topic or concept being studied. Building on their prior knowledge, students work to organize content-specific vocabulary as a before-reading strategy. The List–Group–Label strategy activates students' thinking and prepares them to anticipate what they will read about or see in a science activity. It is also a great formative assessment strategy for teachers to gauge students' prior knowledge.

Using the Strategy with the Reaction in a Bag Activity

During Language-Arts Time

- Before the activity, prepare a list of key terms for the activity, ensuring that most words can fit into categories. Include a few unfamiliar but related terms to challenge students' thinking. You may choose to use the following list for the Reaction in a Bag activity on page 103:

  reaction, expand, contract, dissolve, fizz, bubble, temperature, color, state of matter, gas, liquid, solid, change, calcium chloride, baking soda, bromothymol blue indicator, hot, cold

- Have students identify familiar and unfamiliar words, and provide proper pronunciations for any unfamiliar terms (e.g., calcium chloride, bromothymol blue). Working in pairs, students use the Group–List–Label strategy organizer on page 102 to group words into categories and provide a label for each group that indicates why the words are together or related. All words need to be part of a group. Before you begin the activity, encourage students to pay particular attention to how the words in the Group–List–Label strategy are represented in what they see happening in the activity.

During Science Time

After the activity, provide students with some time to reorganize their lists on the Group–List–Label strategy organizer (page 102), based on what they experienced during the activity. Encourage students to consider their lists and the labels; either can be changed. Prompt students to share why they are changing their lists or labels. Students could then be challenged to use the word list provided to write a summary of the activity.

Variations/Tips/Useful Prompts

If sorting vocabulary in science is new for students, you might want to encourage students to come up with a minimum of three categories for the words in order to expand students' thinking beyond the categories *Words I know* and *Words I don't know*. If students are familiar with a concept or topic, you might want to challenge them to add more words to your list.

The ABCs of Background Knowledge

Activate, Build, Connect

Chemical Reaction: a chemical change that results in new substances being made
- The evidence of new substances being created in the plastic bag is the feeling of warmth (exothermic) or cold (endothermic).

Vocabulary Spotlight

Exothermic, Endothermic
- Root word *therm* means related to heat; prefix *exo–* for a process/reaction that releases heat, rise in temperature; prefix *endo–* for a process that absorbs heat, cools surroundings
- Related words: thermostat, hyperthermic, thermal, thermometer

List–Group–Label

List

Words for the Reaction in a Bag Activity

reaction	color	baking soda
expand	state of matter	bromothymol
contract	gas	blue indicator
dissolve	liquid	hot
fizz	solid	cold
bubble	change	
temperature	calcium chloride	

Group

Use the boxes below to group the words in the list into different categories.

Label

Provide a label or title for each group of words to explain why you grouped them together or how they are related.

Summarize

Use the list of words to summarize what happened in the Reaction in a Bag activity.

Pembroke Publishers ©2023 *Fail-Safe Strategies for Science and Literacy* by Sandra Mirabelli and Lionel Sandner ISBN 978-1-55138-364-4

Reaction in a Bag

Summary

Place two different white substances in opposite corners of a large resealable bag. Place bromothymol blue in a small container and carefully place it in the bag. Seal bag. Mix contents and place on a desk. Observe.

Hints

- In this activity, having the right amounts of substances will ensure a safe activity. Since a gas is produced, monitor how the bag inflates. If too much gas is produced, poke a hole in the bag.
- Calcium chloride is a de-icer and can usually be purchased at a home hardware store.
- Bromothymol blue must be purchased from a science supply house.

Explanation

The bromothymol blue is an indicator dye that turns yellow in the presence of carbon dioxide. When the baking soda and calcium chloride are mixed with the liquid bromothymol blue, a chemical reaction occurs that produces carbon dioxide. The reaction in the bag causes a color change, and the bag inflates to indicate the gas is being produced; if students touch the bag after the reaction has just completed it will be warm, indicating energy being released.

Supplies

- calcium chloride
- baking soda
- bromothymol blue indicator
- small plastic container
- large resealable bag

Preparation

1. Place 5 ml/1 teaspoon of baking soda into one bottom corner of the resealable bag.
2. Place 5 ml/1 teaspoon of calcium chloride in the other bottom corner of the resealable bag.
3. Place 15 ml/1 tablespoon of bromothymol blue into the plastic container and place it in the centre of the resealable bag.
4. Carefully seal the bag, mix the contents by lightly shaking, and place the bag on a desk. The bag should be a safe distance (about 2 m) from students.

Directions

Record your observations and complete the List–Group–Label organizer.

Safety

A gas is being produced in a sealed bag. Stand back to make observations and puncture the bag if it overinflates.

Safe Disposal

Follow handling directions as provided by supplier of bromothymol blue.

STRATEGY #14
Visual Word Sort

Strategy Connections

Thinking Routine: Sort and Classify
Science Activity: Static Action, page 107
When to Use: Before the activity
                 After the activity

The Visual Word Sort strategy combines visual representations of phenomena and concepts with the vocabulary that students will be working with in science. Using this strategy, students are using dual codes or channels (Paivio, 1986; Mayer & Fiorella, 2022) for storing information in their long-term memory (as discussed in Chapter 2). This makes the process of later retrieving the information much easier. Used before an activity or unit, this strategy helps students activate prior knowledge and become familiar with vocabulary they will encounter, while providing teachers with important formative assessment data about students' background knowledge and vocabulary on a particular topic. These visuals and vocabulary can be revisited after the activity to make note of any growth or changes in thinking.

Using the Strategy with the Static Action Activity

During Science Time

- Before engaging in the activity, select vocabulary that relates to the phenomenon that will be investigated. A sample bank of vocabulary that could be used with the Static Action activity on page 107 could include these terms:

    attract, repel, static electricity, electrons, electric force, charged, neutral, energy, gelatin, balloon, stalagmites, charge

- Provide pairs of students with one copy of the Word Sort Cards strategy organizer on page 106 so that they can cut apart the vocabulary cards.
- Prepare a page or placemat with five or six visuals representing various phenomena or concepts related to the vocabulary words. For example, for the Static Action activity, you could include graphics or photos of a young person holding a balloon close to their hair, lightning, a dryer sheet stuck to a sweater, Jello, and a diagram identifying positive and negative charges in two objects.
- Prompt students to consider where they might place each of the vocabulary word cards on the visual placemat. Let students know that some visuals can be described by more than one word from the vocabulary list.
- As students are working with their partners discussing possible connections they can make between words and pictures, walk around the classroom, listening for the background knowledge students will be bringing to the Static Action activity and any terms that are unfamiliar.
- Have students try the science activity. Debrief what happened when the charged balloon was held close to the gelatin. Encourage students to consider some of the vocabulary they encountered in the visual word sort to help them make sense of and explain what happened.

Variations/Tips/Useful Prompts

- It might be helpful to project the placemat of visuals for the whole class to see prior to engaging in the visual word sort. Encourage students to look at each picture on the placemat and share what might be happening, or any experiences they have had with the static electricity situations you have included.

- As students work through the science activity, capture the gelatin interacting with the balloon in a photo you can later post for all to see and discuss.
- After the science activity, make available one set of larger word cards with the same vocabulary as the Visual Word Sort. Post a photo of the gelatin interacting with the balloon for all to see.
- As the class discusses the results, encourage students to connect to the Visual Word Sort vocabulary. When connections are made, students can post the appropriate word card as a label on the projected photo.

During Language-Arts Time

After the Static Action science activity on page 107, present several texts related to static electricity in language-arts time. More challenging texts could become the focus of a teacher read-aloud and accompanying think-aloud, in which you highlight how you are making sense of the text and relating it to the science activity the class engaged in. Some texts could be read by students to further introduce and explain static electricity. Prompt students to notice and share what happens when they encounter a vocabulary word from the Visual Word Sort in the reading passage. Students often say the words tend to light up on the page! Provide time to discuss the text, and have students record definitions and explanations of the vocabulary words in their notebooks, now that they have had several experiences with the words.

The ABCs of Background Knowledge *Activate, Build, Connect*	Vocabulary Spotlight
Static Charge: an imbalance of electric charges on the surface of a material or between materials • The static charge on the balloon induces a charge on the gelatin, causing it to stand up.	*Static* • From Greek root *sta–* meaning "causing to stand" • Antonyms: mobile, active, moving

Word Sort Cards: Static Action Science Activity

Cut along the dotted lines to create separate word cards.

attract	repel	electrons
static electricity	electric force	charged
neutral	gelatin	balloon
energy	stalagmites	charge

Pembroke Publishers ©2023 *Fail-Safe Strategies for Science and Literacy* by Sandra Mirabelli and Lionel Sandner ISBN 978-1-55138-364-4

Static Action

Summary

Sprinkle some gelatin powder on a small square of black paper. Blow up a balloon. Rub the balloon on your hair and bring the balloon close to the gelatin. Observe the tiny gelatin structures that form due to the static field.

Hints

- Make sure the hair being used has minimal product in it.
- The balloon should not touch the gelatin.
- Use round balloons.

Explanation

When you rub a balloon on your hair, charge is transferred to the balloon, and the balloon is statically charged. A common demonstration is to place the balloon on the wall, where it stays in place; this demonstrates that a charged object (the balloon) is attracted to a neutral object (the wall). With gelatin, the grains of powdered gelatin become attracted to the static charge on the balloon. By adjusting the distance between the gelatin and the balloon, you can observe the gelatin structures increase and decrease in size, showing how distance changes the strength of the static electric field.

Supplies

- round balloon
- gelatin package
- 10 cm x 10 cm/4" x 4" squares of black cardboard paper

Directions

1. Blow up a balloon and tie the end.
2. Pour half the packet of gelatin powder onto black cardboard.
3. Rub a balloon on your hair to create a static charge.
4. Bring the charged balloon close to the gelatin powder and observe.

STRATEGY #15
GO with the Flow

Strategy Connections

Thinking Routine: Sort and Classify
Science Activity: What's in a
Mixture?, page 114
When to Use: Before the activity
During the activity
After the activity

The GO (Graphic Organizer) with the Flow strategy supports students in organizing their thoughts and ideas as they work with content from a text or investigation. By having to select the most appropriate type of GO to organize information or their ideas, students use analytical thinking to examine underlying relationships and patterns in the information they will represent. Building depth of knowledge of the different types of graphic organizers (flow, cluster, cycle, and compare-and-contrast organizers) can be helpful across content areas.

Using this Strategy with the What's in a Mixture? Activity

During Language-Arts Time

Use language-arts time to build background knowledge of the four different categories of graphic organizers: flow, cluster, cycle, and compare-and-contrast organizers (see the graphic organizer templates on pages 110–113). Introducing and working with one type of graphic organizer at a time allows students to explore a variety of uses for them. For example,

- You might consider using a cycle GO with a short story or picture book (e.g., *If You Give a Mouse a Cookie*) to emphasize the cyclical structure of the story. In science, students could depict the water or the rock cycle using a cycle organizer.
- Have students use a compare-and-contrast GO to take notes from a science text comparing solutions and mixtures.
- You might encourage students to use a cluster GO to display the various ways to separate a different mixture.
- A cluster GO could also be used to brainstorm real-world examples and applications of solutions and mixtures.

- Challenge students to find examples of the various GOs they come across in a day (e.g., a bus schedule) or find a text that could be summarized using an appropriate GO (e.g., a recipe, an article comparing the latest cell phone to a previous model). Repeated exposure to and use of these four types of graphic organizers can help students brainstorm ideas, take notes when reading, organize ideas to prepare for writing, and better remember information. It's time well-spent, as it supports students' thinking across the curriculum and in a variety of ways.

Variations/Tips/Useful Prompts
Consider having students develop their own GO rather than selecting a premade template.

During Science Time

- Prompt students to write a point-form procedure for separating the mixture they have been presented with in class. Review the four types of graphic organizers introduced in language-arts time with students and encourage them to choose the most appropriate type to represent the steps in their procedure. Provide time for students to meet with a partner and compare their procedures. What similarities and/or differences do they see between their procedure and their partner's procedure? As a class, discuss these similarities and differences, and whether the order of steps matters. In other words, will the order of the steps make a difference to the outcome of separating the mixture?

- Provide time for students to try their procedure with the activity. After the activity, have students check back with their partner to see whether they were both successful in separating the mixture. In a follow-up discussion, have students revisit the initial discussion about whether the order of the steps matters. Students might suggest that some steps can be done at various points without a problem; for example, they might say that the magnet could potentially be used to collect the iron filings before the water is added to create a solution that dissolves the salt. Other steps would be best done in a certain order; for example, students might say it is easiest to pick out the marbles first because they are large in comparison to the other substances. Encourage students to justify their responses by indicating what problems arise if, for example, they add the water to the mixture at the very start.

- Have partners test each other's procedure for separating the mixture as documented in their GO. Students can then provide feedback to each other on whether the steps were clearly articulated and easy to follow. Revisiting the procedure outlined in the GO with their partner after the activity will help students refine their thinking and consider other possible ways to separate the mixture.

The ABCs of Background Knowledge *Activate, Build, Connect*	Vocabulary Spotlight
Separation Techniques: the process of separating out different materials • The separation of the mechanical mixture requires the use of a variety of separation techniques, including hand-picking, dissolving, evaporation, filtration, magnetism.	*Filter* • From Medieval Latin root *filtrum*; chemists used to use the material *felt* to strain liquids, especially when purifying water *Dissolve* • Root word *solve* meaning "loosen, untie, detach, release"; prefix *dis–* meaning "apart, in a different direction" • Prefix *dis–* usually signals that the meaning of the word will be the opposite of the root word • Related words: absolve, resolve

The Flow Graphic Organizer

Purpose:

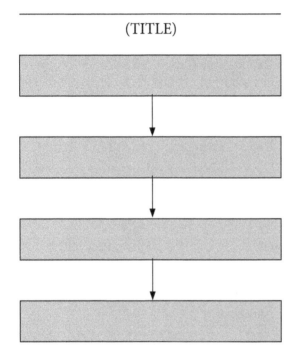

(TITLE)

When I might use this type of graphic organizer:

Examples of where I've seen this organizer used

- at school:

- at home:

- in my day-to-day life:

Pembroke Publishers ©2023 *Fail-Safe Strategies for Science and Literacy* by Sandra Mirabelli and Lionel Sandner ISBN 978-1-55138-364-4

The Cluster Graphic Organizer

Purpose:

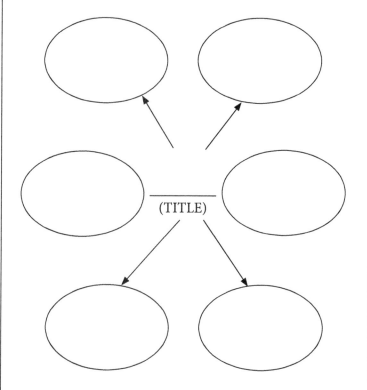

(TITLE)

When I might use this type of graphic organizer:

Examples of where I've seen this organizer used

- at school:

- at home:

- in my day-to-day life:

Pembroke Publishers ©2023 *Fail-Safe Strategies for Science and Literacy* by Sandra Mirabelli and Lionel Sandner ISBN 978-1-55138-364-4

The Cycle Graphic Organizer

Purpose:

_____ (TITLE)

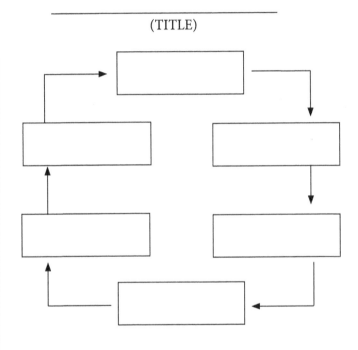

When I might use this type of graphic organizer:

Examples of where I've seen this organizer used

• at school:

• at home:

• in my day-to-day life:

Pembroke Publishers ©2023 *Fail-Safe Strategies for Science and Literacy* by Sandra Mirabelli and Lionel Sandner ISBN 978-1-55138-364-4

The Compare-and-Contrast Graphic Organizer

Purpose:

_____

(TITLE)

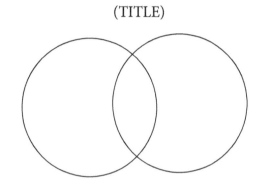

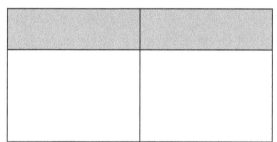

When I might use this type of graphic organizer:

Examples of where I've seen this organizer used

- at school:

- at home:

- in my day-to-day life:

Pembroke Publishers ©2023 *Fail-Safe Strategies for Science and Literacy* by Sandra Mirabelli and Lionel Sandner ISBN 978-1-55138-364-4

What's in a Mixture?

Summary

Students are given a mixture consisting of marbles, sand, salt, and iron filings. They design a procedure for separating out the four different substances, then they carry out their procedure.

Hints

- To make a filter cone, fold a round filter in half twice.
- To evaporate the salt, place the saltwater container in a warm, sunny place and let it sit for a few days. Or you can boil the solution to remove the water. The slower process allows for the creation of salt crystals.
- If sand is in the saltwater solution, refilter it to remove the sand.

Explanation

A mixture is two or more substances combined. For example, soil consists of sand, clay, pebbles, and organic material from nonliving plants and animals. Mechanically separating a mixture means separating the components that make up the mixture. In this activity, students find three different methods for separating the mixture. First, they pick out the larger marbles. Then they add water to the mixture to dissolve the salt and then filter the solution. The remaining mixture has the iron filings removed by a magnet, leaving just the sand.

Supplies

- water
- marbles
- sand
- salt
- iron filings
- filter paper (coffee filters work fine)
- 2 containers
- magnet
- hot plate (optional)

Preparation

1. Create a mixture by mixing together marbles, sand, salt, and iron filings.
2. Give each group of students a sample of the mixture in a small container. You may or may not choose to tell them the number of components in the mixture.

Directions

1. Create a plan to separate out the four substances.
2. Once your plan is approved, carry out your procedure.

What Makes You Say That?

Strategy Connections

Thinking Routine: Analyze and
Interpret
Science Activity: Paper Pot, page 118
When to Use: Before the activity
               After the activity

The What Makes You Say That? strategy (adapted from Ritchhart, Church & Morrison, 2011) prompts students to dig deep in order to identify and articulate the thinking behind their response to a question or situation. This open-ended prompt invites students to elaborate on their response by encouraging them to back up what they say with evidence and reasoning. Used in whole-class discussions, this strategy enriches conversations and allows students to hear differing perspectives as they examine the evidence behind possible explanations. While this strategy is very effective on its own as an oral prompt for conversation, the use of the What Makes You Say That? strategy organizer on page 117 to capture thinking and observations in science will help students work through possible misconceptions.

Using the Strategy with the Paper Pot Activity

During Science Time

- Begin by posing a question related to the activity for students to consider; for example, for the Paper Pot activity on page 118, you can ask, "Can we boil water in a paper cup?" Prompt students to share their answer to this question. It is highly likely that students will answer with a simple yes or no. Most often the response is "No, we can't." To elicit more of the thinking and reasoning behind their response, pose the question, "What makes you say that?" as students share, so the class can hear variations in thinking.

- Prompt students to watch the Paper Pot activity on page 118 closely and record as many observations as they can. For example, they can note where the candle flame is touching the cup and the length of time the flame and the cup are in contact, in addition to other changes to the materials (the cup, the water) over time.

- Have students revisit their initial response to the focus question about boiling water in a paper cup and identify whether they were correct or incorrect in their thinking. Many students will find they were incorrect. This activity reveals a common misconception that you can't heat water in a paper cup because paper is very flammable. Students expect the cup to burn, just as it would if it were empty. However, in this case, the presence of water in the cup absorbs the heat energy.

- Provide time for students to select observations to use as evidence that indicates they were either correct or incorrect in their initial thinking. Ultimately, whether they were correct or incorrect, they can cite the same evidence: *the paper cup did not burn*; *the water did warm up or boil if left that long*. If students have background knowledge of heat transfer or the boiling point of water and the burning point for paper, encourage them to connect to and use scientific vocabulary and principles in their reasoning as the class discusses this discrepant event. After the conversation, it is important for students to explain and make note of the science behind this activity as a visual way to correct their misconception.

Variations/Tips/Useful Prompts

- The What Makes You Say That? strategy can be used across the curriculum to prompt students to share their thinking and how they are connecting it to their responses. It is easily combined with other strategies during oral conversations.
- You might find that students have difficulty distinguishing between evidence and reasoning. Remind students that evidence will come from their observations or what they saw. By explaining what the observations mean or why they are significant and related to the question being asked, they are providing reasoning.
- While this strategy is easily implemented as a teacher prompt in oral conversations, the value of tracking thinking throughout the activity is that it provides a record for students to see the change in their thinking.

During Language-Arts Time

The *What makes you say that?* prompt is useful in all subject areas as a way to encourage students to elaborate on their responses. In language arts, you can use it to encourage students to share why they assign certain personality traits to the main character, for example, or to elaborate on what motivates a character to act in a certain way. Another useful open-ended prompt that encourages students to share more of their thinking is *Tell me more…*

The ABCs of Background Knowledge *Activate, Build, Connect*	Vocabulary Spotlight
Heat Transfer: the movement of thermal energy from an area of warm to cool • The cup does not catch on fire because thermal energy from the flame transfers to the paper and then to the water. The paper never gets hot enough to burn.	*Capacity* • Root word from Latin *capax* meaning "able to hold much"; suffix *–ity* means "quality of" • Related words: capability, capable

What Makes You Say That?

Can we boil water in a paper cup?

Yes _____ No _____

What makes you say that?

Your Observations:

Was your initial thinking correct? _____ or incorrect? _____

What makes you say that?
Use the chart below to record specific observations from the activity that explain why your initial thinking was correct or incorrect.

Evidence #1	Evidence #2

What scientific principle(s) help explain what actually happened?

Pembroke Publishers ©2023 *Fail-Safe Strategies for Science and Literacy* by Sandra Mirabelli and Lionel Sandner ISBN 978-1-55138-364-4

Paper Pot

Summary

Fill a paper cup with water. Place a lighted candle under it so the flame is touching only the part of the paper cup that has water on the other side. The paper cup doesn't catch fire! But you do see black carbon build-up where the flame touched the cup.

Hints

- Place the flame only where there is water in the cup.

Explanation

Usually a flame is sufficient to cause paper to combust. When there is water on one side of the cup, the thermal energy is transferred through the paper and into the water. This means the paper does not burn.

Supplies

- paper cup
- water
- candle
- matches or a lighter

Directions

1. Fill a paper cup 7/8 full of water.
2. Light a candle.
3. While holding the cup with one hand, take the candle and place it directly under the cup. Ensure the flame touches the cup where there is water inside.
4. Observe.

Safety

Follow your school board's safety policy related to use of open flame in the classroom.

Connect Two

Strategy Connections

Thinking Routine: Analyze and Interpret
Science Activity: Flying Tea Bag, page 122
When to Use: After the activity

The Connect Two strategy encourages students to engage in analytical thinking, as they look for similarities and differences to connect two concepts or ideas. As students work to identify how their two chosen concepts are related, they build a concept map in their heads that deepens and strengthens their understanding of both concepts. This strategy prompts students to actively search for patterns and relationships between two concepts and helps them to remember more information.

Using the Strategy with the Flying Tea Bag Activity

During Science Time

- After the activity has been experienced, prompt students to choose two concepts or terms from a short list you provide; for example, for the Flying Tea Bag activity on page 122, the list might include the following terms:

  convection current, conduction, radiation, heat transfer, air molecules, oxygen, fuel, energy, flame, rise

  Using the space provided on the Connect Two strategy organizer on page 121, have students write a sentence or two that explains how or why the two terms they have chosen are connected. Encourage students to use what was seen and discussed in the Flying Tea Bag activity, as well as their background knowledge, to support the connections they are making.
- Students can use the subsequent spaces on the strategy organizer either to find another way the first two terms or concepts are connected or to choose two new concepts from the list to connect.
- Have students share their connections with a partner or debrief the strategy responses as a whole class.

Variations/Tips/Useful Prompts

- It might be helpful to model this strategy with the whole class before prompting students to work individually. For example, you could explain the similarities and differences between a *demo* or *demonstration* and an *experiment* in science, and proceed to write a few sentences about how these two types of investigations in science are connected:

  A demo and an experiment both involve hands-on learning using specific materials. A demonstration usually shows how something works, while a science experiment usually tests a variable to see how or why it affects something else.

- To support the variety of learners in your classroom, it can be beneficial to review what students understand about some of the terms or concepts in the list before working to connect them. After finding a similarity that connects two terms, challenge students to also explain how these terms differ.

During Language-Arts Time

- Introduce students to the four types of strategy organizers that are particularly useful in science: flow charts, cycle organizers, cluster organizers, and compare-and-contrast organizers; see strategy #15 GO with the Flow and templates on pages 110–113. To link to the Connect Two strategy, focus students' attention on organizers, such as Venn diagrams and T-charts, used to compare and contrast things. Explain that the Connect Two strategy is about explaining the middle of the Venn diagram or how two concepts are similar or related.
- Consider building background knowledge on the concept of heat transfer and how we experience it in everyday life by bringing in supplementary texts on the concept to read together or for students to read on their own. To connect to the Flying Tea Bag activity, provide a passage on different ways to transfer heat and have students use either a three-way Venn diagram or three-column chart to compare and contrast *convection*, *conduction*, and *radiation*. Once more knowledge has been built with other reading passages on the concept of heat transfer, students can choose a different type of strategy organizer to organize the information from the text or their growing knowledge of heat transfer.

The ABCs of Background Knowledge *Activate, Build, Connect*	Vocabulary Spotlight
Temperature: degree of hotness or coldness of an object measured on a scale; the average moving (kinetic) energy of particles within a system • Lighting the tea bag increases the temperature of the tea bag. The resulting heat transfers to the air particles, making them move faster and spread farther apart, and creating less-dense air that rises. The newly created convection current causes the last piece of the tea bag to rise.	*Temperature* • From Latin *temperare* meaning "to mix different conditions,"; e.g., hot and cold, dry and humid • Related words: temperate, temperament

Connect Two: Flying Tea Bag Activity

List of Terms

convection current	air molecules	flame
conduction	oxygen	rise
radiation	fuel	
heat transfer	energy	

Example: *Convection* and *radiation* are connected because they both transfer thermal energy through the atmosphere. However, *conduction* transfers thermal energy through a conducting material.

_____ and _____ are connected

because _____

_____

_____

_____ and _____ are connected

because _____

_____

_____

_____ and _____ are connected

because _____

_____

_____

Flying Tea Bag

Summary

Most tea bags with a string are actually folded cylinders of paper. Using one of these tea bags, remove the staple and empty out the tea leaves. Form a cylinder with the bag and place it upright on a clean table with nothing on it. Light the top of the tea bag and observe the tea bag fly up in the air like a ghost.

Hints

- Table surface must be flat and, ideally, metal. A pie plate on the table can work well.
- Ensure there is no air flow from fans or vents blowing onto the table.
- Have fire safety equipment nearby and no flammable material on the table.

Explanation

When the tea bag burns almost to the bottom, its mass is small enough to be pulled up in the convection current created by the tea bag as it burns.

Supplies

- tea bag (the kind that, when empty, forms a cylinder)
- matches
- fire safety equipment

Directions

1. Unpack a tea bag by removing the staple and emptying out tea leaves.
2. Place the cylinder tea bag upright on a table or metal pie plate.
3. Light tea bag at the top of the cylinder.
4. Observe.

Safety

Follow your school board's safety policy related to use of open flame in the classroom.

Take Note

Strategy Connections

Thinking Routine: Analyze and Interpret
Science Activity: Glowing Spice, page 125
When to Use: After the activity

The Take Note strategy (adapted from Ritchhart and Church, 2020) provides students with an opportunity to reflect on an activity and identify key issues and questions they have after the learning event has taken place. Prompts in this strategy encourage students to analyze confusing and challenging parts of an activity and provide teachers feedback to help identify where support and further knowledge-building is necessary.

Using the Strategy with the Glowing Spice Activity

During Science Time

- After doing the Glowing Spice activity, distribute a copy of the Take Note strategy organizer on page 124 to students.
- Prompt students to *take note* of the following:

  > What did you find interesting or unexpected in this activity?
  > Have you seen a reaction like this before? Where? When?
  > What did you find confusing about the reaction in this activity?
  > What questions would you like to discuss or explore further as a result of this activity?
  > What important things have you learned about turmeric in this activity?

- Have students share what they have written with other group members and discuss, with the intention of clearing up any confusion and helping each other make sense of the reaction, or to spark curiosity and interest in further exploration or investigation.

Variations/Tips/Useful Prompts

You might consider giving students the alternative of using index cards or a digital platform to capture notes. It is important that the method chosen allows students an opportunity to trade notes and comment on one another's responses.

During Language-Arts Time

- A strategy for oral conversation that involves students meeting around the classroom for short periods of time would also be a great after-activity opportunity for them to discuss and build on each other's learning. In each round of conversation, students can share their answers to one of the questions with a partner and take note of their partner's answer when it helps them further elaborate on their own.
- Provide time for students to research and build more knowledge of *chemiluminescence* and of *bioluminescence*, which is a form of chemiluminescence where light is emitted by living things, such as fireflies, some jellyfish and other deep sea marine animals, and some types of fungi and bacteria.

The ABCs of Background Knowledge

Activate, Build, Connect

Chemiluminescence: the emission of light during a chemical reaction
- The UV light energy interacts with the turmeric, causing the spice to glow.

Vocabulary Spotlight

Chemiluminescence
- Prefix *chemi–* meaning "having to do with chemicals, chemical reaction"; root word *luminare* meaning "to light up"
- Related words: bioluminescence, luminescent, illuminate

Take Note

What did you find interesting or unexpected in this activity? Explain how/why.

Have you seen a reaction like this before? When? Where?

What did you find confusing about this activity?

What questions would you like to discuss or explore as a result of this activity?

What important things have you learned about turmeric in this activity?

Pembroke Publishers ©2023 *Fail-Safe Strategies for Science and Literacy* by Sandra Mirabelli and Lionel Sandner ISBN 978-1-55138-364-4

Glowing Spice

Summary

Darken the classroom. Shine an ultraviolet light on a clear glass of rubbing alcohol. Sprinkle turmeric spice in the rubbing alcohol. Observe the fluorescence.

Hints

- Ultraviolet flashlights can be purchased at a hardware store.
- Fluorescence is also observed when ultraviolet light is shone on tonic water.

Explanation

Fluorescence is caused when a substance receives enough radiant energy from another source to make the substance particles begin to vibrate faster. For the substance particles to return to their resting state, the energy must be given off. The emitted light has a lower energy and wavelength than the incoming radiation. The result is a visible glow of the material. In this example, the turmeric spice contains an ultraviolet fluorescent substance called curcumin. The turmeric is exposed to ultraviolet light energy that excites the curcumin. The resulting release of energy causes the turmeric to fluoresce or glow. This fluorescence phenomenon can occur naturally or be induced chemically.

Supplies

- turmeric spice in powder form
- UV flashlight (available from a hardware store)
- rubbing alcohol (99%)
- 100 ml beaker or small, clear plastic container

Directions

1. Pour rubbing alcohol to fill the beaker or container to three quarters full.
2. Darken the room.
3. Shine the UV flashlight onto the beaker or container.
4. Sprinkle the turmeric powder into the beaker or container.
5. Observe.

3-D GO

Strategy Connections

Thinking Routine: Analyze and Interpret
Science Activity: How Big? How Small?, page pages 130–131
When to Use: After the activity

A Foldable™(Zike, 2008) is a student-made, three-dimensional graphic organizer (3-D GO) designed to help learners organize and better understand new concepts. By folding a paper in half, adding cuts to create tabs, and labeling these tabs with key concepts and vocabulary, students interact with new learning in a fun way. Further information related to each key concept can be added under the appropriate tabs. These 3-D GOs offer students a visual way to chunk information into sections as a method of note-taking in science and other subject areas. 3-D GOs can easily be added to student notebooks as an interactive element.

Using the Strategy with the How Big? How Small? Activity

During Science Time

- After doing the How Big? How Small? activity on pages 130–131, guide students in making a seven-tab 3-D GO; see template on page 128 and sample below. Have students record each of the units they worked with in the activity on the front of the 3-D GO: *nano–, micro–, milli–, centi–, kilo–, mega–, giga–.* Encourage students to present these units from smallest to largest or largest to smallest on the front of their 3-D GO. Inside the 3-D GO, students can provide information that helps them remember the scale of each unit. For example, students can draw or name objects or living things that would be measured using each unit, and represent the unit using powers of ten and exponents: *nano* could be described inside the 3-D GO as

  - one billionth
  - 0.000000001
  - 10^{-9}

Students can add that this unit would be appropriate to measure extremely small objects, such as atoms and molecules:

> Scientists would use nanometers (nm) to measure these objects. If measuring the speed of an electronic device like a computer, scientists would use nanoseconds (ns).

Sample Seven-Tab 3-D GO with How Big? How Small? Terms

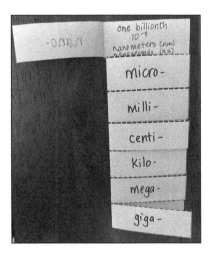

Sample Three-Tab 3-D GO as a Venn Diagram

During Language-Arts Time

- During language-arts time, 3-D GOs can be used to support and reinforce how words are constructed. Explain that many commonly used words are made up of a root word and an affix. An affix is a group of letters that come either at the beginning of a word (a prefix) or at the end of a word (a suffix) and add meaning or change the meaning of the root word. Some prefixes that are commonly encountered in science are *uni–, di–, tri–, mono–, poly–*. Students can set up a vertical 3-D GO with five tabs for these prefixes on the front. Inside, students can define what each prefix means and brainstorm a variety of words that start in these ways. Many connections to math vocabulary can also be made with this particular set of prefixes. Discussing and sharing the words they include in their 3-D GO can help students expand their vocabulary. Be sure to discuss how the prefix influences each word's meaning and helps us define whole groups of related words; for example *uni–* meaning "one" is present in the words *universe, unicycle, unify, uniform, unison,* and *union.*
- Depending on the current unit of study in science, you might select other prefixes to examine and create word families. For example, in studying ecosystems, the prefixes *eco–, photo–, herb–,* and *carn–* would be appropriate. Similarly 3-D GOs could assist students in looking at common suffixes encountered in science: e.g., *–ology, –phyll, –synthesis, –sphere, –vore.*

Variations/Tips/Useful Prompts

3-D GOs can be used to take notes on various topics or concepts, as in the How Big? How Small? activity on pages 130–131, but also consider using them to compare and contrast concepts. For example, a three-tab 3-D GO could be created with students prior to this activity, depicting a Venn diagram on the front and used by students to compare and contrast the terms *micro–* and *macro–* inside. The middle tab in the three-tab 3-D GO would be where the two circles in the Venn diagram intersect. See sample below and the 3-Tab 3-D GO as a Venn Diagram template on page 129.

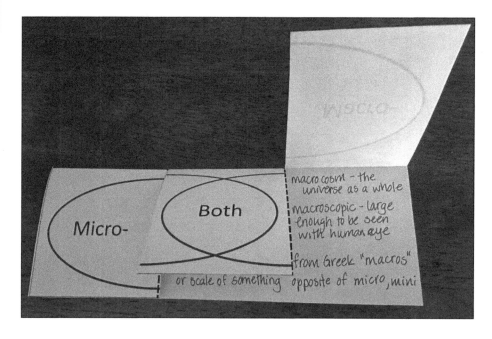

7-Tab 3-D GO Template

Cut out the table. Write terms in the column on the Outside Front of the 3-D GO. Fold the table in half vertically along the bolded middle line. Cut along the dotted lines to the halfway point (the fold line) to create flip-up tabs that reveal space underneath for you to make notes.

Outside Back	Fold Line	Outside Front

Pembroke Publishers ©2023 *Fail-Safe Strategies for Science and Literacy* by Sandra Mirabelli and Lionel Sandner ISBN 978-1-55138-364-4

3-Tab 3-D GO as a Venn Diagram

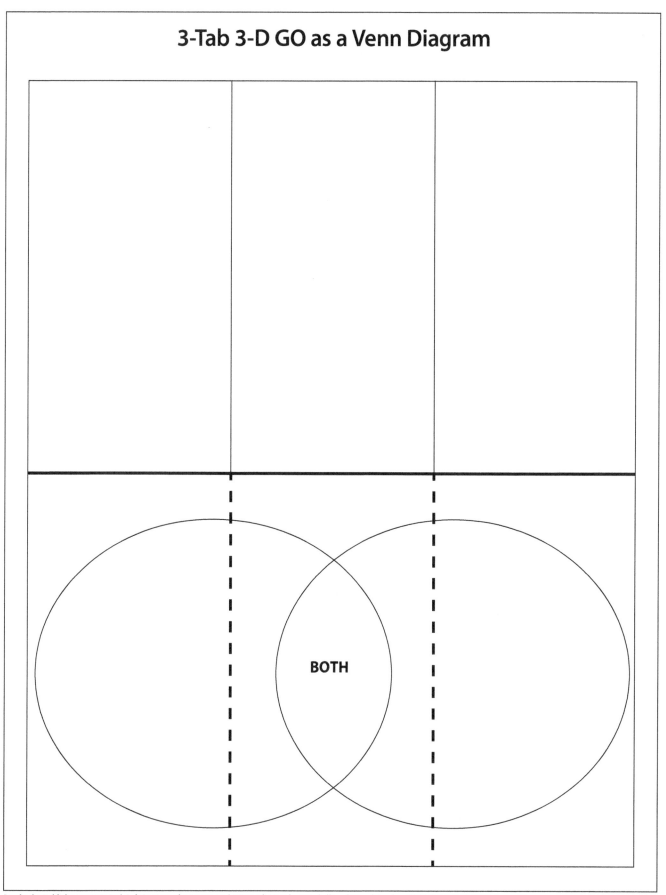

BOTH

Pembroke Publishers ©2023 *Fail-Safe Strategies for Science and Literacy* by Sandra Mirabelli and Lionel Sandner ISBN 978-1-55138-364-4

How Big? How Small?

Summary

This activity presents six questions that give students an opportunity to work with units and scale. Three questions on big units and numbers using a number line and facts; three questions on small units and numbers using a number line and real-life examples. The goal of this activity is to make students comfortable with units and appreciate the difference in scale between the units.

Hint

- This activity can be set up as stations where students work through the Big Units questions and then the Small Units questions.

Supplies for Stations

- cue cards with the questions
- paper for answers

Teacher Directions

1. Present the questions to your class.
2. Identify and support misunderstandings as needed.

Big Units

Question 1: How Big?

Have an envelope of slips of paper with the terms shown in the table. Students remove the slips from the envelope and arrange them to create a table similar to the one below. The purpose of this activity is to have students think about and visually connect the unit to the exponent and mathematical definition.

Giga	10^9	Billion
Mega	10^6	Million
Kilo	10^3	Thousand

Question 2: Million vs Billion

On the number line, where would you place *Million*?

1   Billion

Question 3: Crazy Facts

- How many seconds in a million? How many days is this?
- How many seconds in a billion? How many days is this?

Small Units

Question 4: How Small?

Have an envelope of slips of paper with the terms shown in the table. Students remove the slips from the envelope and arrange them to create a table similar to the one below. The purpose of this activity is to have students think about and visually connect the unit to the exponent and mathematical definition.

Nano	10^{-9}	Billionth
Micro	10^{-6}	Millionth
Milli	10^{-3}	Thousandth
Centi	10^{-2}	Hundredth

Question 5: Small Number Line

Which side of the number line do small units like *nano*, *micro*, and *milli* get placed? Approximately where?

| -1 | 0 | 1 |

Question 6: Matching in Real Life

1. Match the unit to real-life things. Put terms on slips of paper and mix.

Nano	Virus
Micro	Bacteria
Milli	Salt Crystal

2. Have students remove the slips from the envelope and use them to create a table.

Frayer Model

Strategy Connections
Thinking Routine: Analyze and Interpret
Science Activity: A Busy Cup of Science, page 135
When to Use: Before the activity
            After the activity

The Frayer Model is a graphic organizer that helps students build a deeper understanding of key vocabulary connected to new concepts they are reading about, viewing, or experiencing. Using this four-part chart, pairs, groups, or individuals can apply what they've learned to define a key term or concept, outline key characteristics, and give examples and non-examples. The four-part structure of the Frayer Model can also be used before an activity to engage students in a discussion that activates prior knowledge.

Using the Strategy with the A Busy Cup of Science Activity

During Science Time

- There are two important terms connected to the A Busy Cup of Science activity on page 135 that will benefit from deeper analysis using a Frayer Model: *density* and *chemical change*. Modelling how to use a Frayer Model with the first term—*density*—will help students working in pairs or small groups analyze the second term—*chemical change*—after the activity.
- As you introduce the science activity, highlight that there are two concepts connected to this activity that you will explore. Post a paper chart or electronic version of the Frayer Model for *density*, explaining that the four parts of the Frayer Model can be used as a structure or guide for thinking to develop a deep understanding of the concept of density.
- Post some photos of objects sinking and floating in a liquid and/or a density column. Ask students to turn and talk about the photos and explain how these photos show density. Use students' thinking to fill in various parts of the Frayer Model as they are offered: *density relates to whether a substance is sinking or floating; oil is less dense than water so it floats on water; it measures how tightly packed molecules are in a given volume of an object; solids are usually more dense than liquids.* Explain that, as you work through the activity, more can be added to the Frayer Model on density; in fact, sometimes it is easiest to save the definition of the term for last: *You can consider our current definition of density as a working definition, in case we want to add more or clarify it after the activity.*
- After doing the activity, return to the Frayer Model and ask students if there is anything more they would add to the definition, characteristics, examples, and non-examples. This would also be the time to revise any entries that need clarification or adjustment, or that were misconceptions.
- Introduce the Frayer Model strategy organizer on page 134 as a template for students to make a personal copy of the class Frayer Model on density. Working with a partner, students proceed to create a Frayer Model for the second term, the *chemical change* witnessed in this activity. Remind students that they saw the same chemical change between the baking soda and vinegar in the Dancing Raisins activity (page 62). Have students share their ideas for *chemical change* to add to a class Frayer Model. This can eventually be posted as part of a science word wall.

During Language-Arts Time

- Use the Frayer Model with terms students already know as an introduction to the strategy; for example, you could examine the prefix *pre–* meaning "before." Begin by having students brainstorm words they know that start with this prefix, as examples to help set context as you move on to build the various parts of the Frayer Model: *prepay, previous, prepare, preview, precaution.* This initial use of the Frayer model will build comfort with its parts so that students can move on to unfamiliar or more-complex terms later.
- Consider using this strategy to explore words that denote a character's personality traits (e.g., open-minded, obstinate) in a book the class is reading. Key concepts and content from other subject areas—such as math terms like *polygons* or *integers*; visual art terms like *value, perspective*; or drama terms like *tableau*—would also work with the Frayer Model strategy.

Variations/Tips/Useful Prompts

- Students can start in any quadrant of the Frayer Model. The definition does not have to be completed first. It is sometimes helpful to have students connect to their background knowledge and start by offering examples or non-examples of a term as a way to get discussion going.
- Consider prompting students to add

  - photos or illustrations to visualize the word
  - related terms in a web around the key word
  - the part of speech under the key word
  - synonyms to help build vocabulary
  - antonyms to help clarify and define the boundaries of the word

The ABCs of Background Knowledge *Activate, Build, Connect*	Vocabulary Spotlight
Density: a measurement of how tightly materials are packed together in a given volume • Vegetable oil floats on water because it is less dense.	*Density* • Root word from Latin *densus* meaning "very close or compact"; can also mean "thick, crowded" • Related words: dense, condense

Frayer Models
Defining *Density* and *Chemical Change*

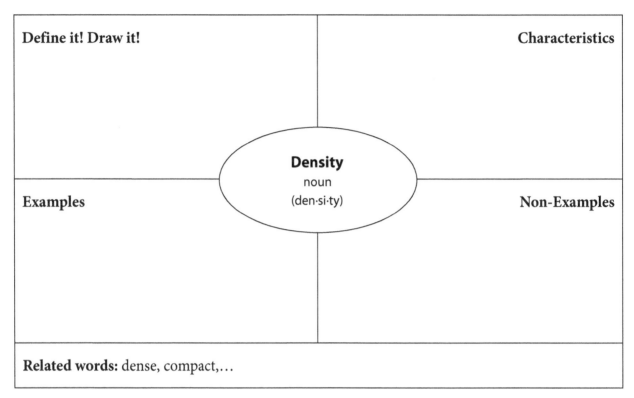

Define it! Draw it!

Characteristics

Density
noun
(den·si·ty)

Examples

Non-Examples

Related words: dense, compact,...

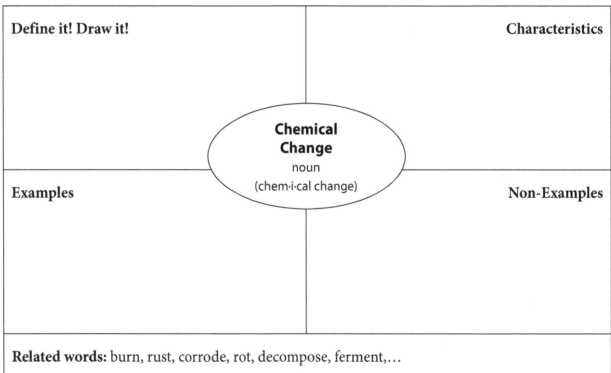

Define it! Draw it!

Characteristics

Chemical Change
noun
(chem·i·cal change)

Examples

Non-Examples

Related words: burn, rust, corrode, rot, decompose, ferment,...

Pembroke Publishers ©2023 *Fail-Safe Strategies for Science and Literacy* by Sandra Mirabelli and Lionel Sandner ISBN 978-1-55138-364-4

A Busy Cup of Science

Summary

A plastic cup with baking soda on the bottom and vegetable oil on top creates the conditions for a chemical change when colored vinegar is added. The acidic vinegar reacts with the baking soda to produce carbon dioxide gas. The gas attaches to the surface of the vinegar, causing the drops to rise.

Hint

- When adding vegetable oil, tip the cup sideways and pour slowly so as not to disturb the baking soda.

Explanation

Baking soda and vegetable oil are layered in a cup, and drops of colored vinegar are added. The vinegar is denser than oil and will sink to the bottom. Oil and vinegar do not mix, so the vinegar drops form spheres as they fall through the oil to the bottom, where the vinegar and baking soda begin to react to form carbon dioxide gas. The gas bubbles attach to the surface of the vinegar bubble and lift the vinegar to the surface. At the surface, the gas is released and the vinegar bubble falls back down.

Supplies

- plastic cup or beaker
- vegetable oil (125 ml/¼ cup)
- baking soda (15 g/1 tablespoon)
- vinegar (20 ml/one dropper)
- food coloring
- eye dropper

Directions

1. Place 15 g/1 tablespoon baking soda in the bottom of the cup.
2. Carefully pour in enough vegetable oil until the cup is half full, about 125 ml/ 1/4 cup.
3. Add food coloring to a small amount of vinegar.
4. Slowly add drops of colored vinegar to the cup.
5. Observe and fill out Frayer Model student organizer.

I Used to Think… But Now I Think…

The I Used to Think… But Now I Think… strategy engages students in reflective thinking, as they examine how and why their perceptions and beliefs might have changed as a result of new learning. Both phases of the strategy occur after the learning experience, prompting students to recall and compare their originally held ideas or perceptions to the knowledge they currently hold. This strategy provides an opportunity for students to engage in metacognition and for teachers to collect formative assessment data to inform further instruction.

Using the Strategy with the Toilet Paper Rope Activity

During Science Time

- Begin by focusing students' attention on the purpose of this strategy. For example, with the Toilet Paper Rope activity on page 138, explain that they already know a lot about the physical properties of toilet paper. Prompt students to think about what they had expected to happen when you try to lift something using a rope made of toilet paper. Have students record this idea in the first box on the I Used to Think… But Now I Think… strategy organizer on page 137, under the I Used to Think… head; for example, students might write, *I used to think… toilet paper is really flimsy.*
- Prompt students to think about how their thinking has changed as a result of doing the activity. Did something unexpected or surprising happen that they were not expecting? Have students reread their I Used to Think… statement and consider how their thinking has changed. In the second box on the strategy organizer, have students explain what they now think; for example, students might finish the example above by stating, *But now I think… that there are ways to change or manipulate a weak material like toilet paper to make it stronger.*

Variations/Tips/Useful Prompts

- It is important to model the use of this strategy with the whole class so that students become accustomed to the amount of explanation to provide. Consider including this strategy in oral conversation in other subject areas so that this will not be the first time students encounter it.
- Have students post their responses to this sentence stem in a shared document online or on chart paper in the classroom for everyone to see changes in thinking.

During Language-Arts Time

Model and engage students in using the *I used to think… but now I think…* sentence stem with a variety of texts you are reading, from picture books to poetry or novels. For example, you might discuss how the reader's perception of a character in a short story changes as a result of an event or interaction with another character using the *I used to think… but now I think…* stem. This modelling will support students in recognizing that our thinking does change and that it is important to reflect on and analyze why it does.

The ABCs of Background Knowledge

Activate, Build, Connect

Properties: characteristics that enable us to differentiate one material from another
- Modifications to the properties of a material can create novel uses; e.g., layering and twisting toilet paper creates a rope.

Vocabulary Spotlight

Laminate
- From Latin *lamina* meaning "a thin sheet of metal or other materials"
- It refers to a material made of thin layers.
- Related words: lamination, laminated

I Used to Think… But Now I Think…

I used to think…

But now I think…

I used to think…

But now I think…

Pembroke Publishers ©2023 *Fail-Safe Strategies for Science and Literacy* by Sandra Mirabelli and Lionel Sandner ISBN 978-1-55138-364-4

A New Kind of Rope

Summary

Place two students about 3 m/10 ft apart and hand one of them a roll of toilet paper. Have the students pass the roll back and forth until all the paper is used. The layers of toilet paper should lie evenly on top of each other. When the roll is done, have students fold the layered toilet paper in half; you might have to help them. Have them repeat the fold two or three times, then twist the paper. You now have toilet paper rope. Test the strength of the rope!

Hints

- Keep the layers of paper flat and on top of each other.
- After you have made your toilet paper rope, fold it one more time.
- Don't twist the toilet paper rope too tightly or it will start to break at the perforations.

Explanation

Any material can be designed to meet a specific function. Toilet paper is soft and is used for… well, you know. But that same material can be redesigned to meet a different function. By layering and twisting the toilet paper, you create a strong rope of an initially soft material.

Supplies

- one roll of toilet paper

Teacher Directions

1. Have two students stand 3 to 4 m/10 to 12 ft apart
2. Have a third student take the end of the toilet paper and pass the roll to the other student, who holds the paper at the roll.
3. The roll is taken back and forth between the students until the roll is empty. Make sure the paper layers are smooth and on top of each other.
4. Have students fold paper until it is 2 to 3 m in length.
4. Have students twist paper several turns, but not enough to break the perforations between squares.
5. Students fold the paper rope one more time.
6. Test the strength of the rope created by pulling and lifting.

3–2–1 Exit Card

Strategy Connections

Thinking Routine: Conclude and Apply

Science Activity: Water Screen, page 141

When to Use: After the activity

The 3–2–1 Exit Card strategy provides a structure for students to summarize their learning after a lesson or activity. Prompts can be varied to suit the learning experience so that students can describe what they took away from the learning situation. This strategy provides informal formative assessment data for teachers that can assist them in assessing understanding, planning further instruction, identifying misconceptions, and gauging student interest in a topic or activity.

Using the Strategy with the Water Screen Activity

During Science Time

The Water Screen activity on page 141 offers an opportunity to work on the science skill of identifying and manipulating variables and on the concept of a *fair test* in science.

- After participating in the Water Screen activity on page 141 and a debriefing discussion, have students use the 3–2–1 Exit Card strategy organizer on page 140 to write three observations they made during the activity, two ways they might change one of the materials in the activity to see if it would yield the same result (e.g., temperature of water, size of holes in the screen, amount of water in the container), and one thing they found interesting and want to explore further about water or its behavior as a result of this activity.
- Facilitate a discussion of all the ways the materials could be changed to see if they would get the same result. Emphasize that, in order to conduct a fair test, you would make only one change to a material at any one time.

The ABCs of Background Knowledge

Activate, Build, Connect

Properties of Water: Water has a high surface tension that causes the outer layer of liquid to act like a skin.
- The high surface tension of water combined with the small holes in the mesh prevent water from going through.

Variations/Tips/Useful Prompts

- The 3–2–1 Exit Card most commonly prompts students to identify three things they've learned, two things that were interesting, and one question they have. These prompts can easily be changed to suit your learning objectives and intentions. For example, you could prompt students for three observations they made, two wonderings they have as a result of what happened, and one way they could change this activity to test a new question.
- Exit cards can be thought of as ticket out the door at the end of class. However, you might also consider having small groups of students complete and present their 3–2–1 list to the class.

Vocabulary Spotlight

Mesh
- From Old English *masc* (pronounced "mash") meaning "the open spaces in a net or netting"
- Related words: enmesh, intermesh, unmesh

During Language-Arts Time

Provide all groups in the class with a small selection of anonymous class exit cards. Prompt students to work together to collate responses from the various exit cards they have by looking for commonalities and differences. Have each group present their summaries of the exit card responses to the class.

3–2–1 Exit Card Strategy: Water Screen Activity

3 observations I made during this activity:

2 ways I can change one of the materials in this activity to see if I will get the same result:

1 thing about water and/or its behavior that I would like to explore further:

Pembroke Publishers ©2023 *Fail-Safe Strategies for Science and Literacy* by Sandra Mirabelli and Lionel Sandner ISBN 978-1-55138-364-4

Water Screen

Summary

Fill a mason jar with water and cover with a small mesh screen. Invert the jar and the water doesn't flow through the screen. Water can behave strangely at times.

Hint

- Mesh screens can be purchased at a home improvement store.

Explanation

In chemical terms, water is a polar liquid. In real life, this means that water can be sticky. Another way of describing this phenomenon is to describe water as having high surface tension. When you fill a glass with water, you'll notice the water "climbs" or sticks slightly up the sides of the glass, due to the high surface tension. The same situation occurs when water is trying to flow through the mesh screen. The water sticks to the sides of the mesh and prevents water from flowing. If you touch the mesh, you break the surface tension, and the water will flow.

Supplies

- water
- mason jar with canning lid
- mesh screen (enough to cover the top of the mason jar)

Directions

1. Completely fill a mason jar with water.
2. Place mesh screen over top of jar and screw the lid back on. Use only the ring of the mason jar lid so the screen is exposed.
3. Invert the jar and observe.

STRATEGY #23
5 W's and a How

Strategy Connections

Thinking Routine: Conclude and Apply

Science Activity: Better Paper Towel, page 145

When to Use: Before the activity
After the activity

The 5 W's and a How Strategy supports students in drawing a conclusion from a phenomenon, concept, or issue, and in applying that learning to a broader context. Creating 5 W questions (who, what, when, where, why) and a How question, all of which which require more than a yes or no answer, prompts students to gather information for problem-solving. A How question can also be used as an overarching focus question that prompts students to apply their experience in an activity to suggest solutions. This strategy helps students draw conclusions from their findings in an activity and apply that learning to consider the significance of the phenomenon being studied in a broader context.

Using the Strategy with the Better Paper Towel Activity

During Science Time

- Prior to doing the Better Paper Towel activity on page 145, ask students to share their experiences with the absorbency of different types of paper towels and, as a result, how much paper towel they use. For example, they might share that they think the paper towel they use at home absorbs more water than the paper towel they use at school, so they use less of it at home.
- Share that the science activity will have them focus on the question *How can we rethink or redesign paper towels to reduce waste?* Explain that this question will help focus their thinking as they investigate the effectiveness of different hand-drying techniques when using paper towels.
- Present the Zero Waste Hierarchy model found on the 5 W's and a How strategy organizer on page 144. Explain that the model was designed to add more depth to the internationally recognized 3 R's (reduce, reuse, recycle) model which students are familiar with. The Zero Waste International Alliance defines zero waste as

    …the Conservation of all resources by means of responsible production, consumption, reuse, and recovery of all products, packaging, and materials without burning them and with no discharges to land, water, or air that threaten the environment or human health.
    (Version 8.0 updated May 19, 2022; retrieved from: https://zwia.org/zwh/)

    Share that this model encourages governments and industry to develop policies and practices that move up the hierarchy toward a zero waste status that properly manages resources and looks to reduce environmental impact. Explain that you will keep this model in mind as you look for a part to play in moving to zero waste.
- Prompt students to use 5 W's and a How to create questions they have about paper towel waste while considering the Zero Waste Hierarchy. For example, students might ask: *When were paper towels invented and why? Who uses the most paper towels? Why can't we recycle paper towels? Why are paper towels bad for the environment? How can we reduce paper towel use?*
- Introduce the Better Paper Towel science activity on page 145 and have students track the effectiveness of their hand-drying techniques on the 5 W's and a How strategy organizer on page 144. Discuss the results of the activity,

emphasizing any differences they noticed. Share the science behind how paper towels absorb water, highlighting that water is attracted to the cellulose that makes up the fibres in the paper towel and we know water likes to stick together (also seen in the Drops of Water on a Coin activity on page 57). So the water follows other water already filling the spaces between fibres. Folding the paper towel creates more spaces for the water to fill.

- Prompt students to return to their 5 W's and a How questions to see if any of their questions have been answered. Discuss ideas students have about how we can rethink or redesign paper towels to move toward zero waste as a result of engaging in the Better Paper Towel activity.

Variations/Tips/Useful Prompts

- If all attempts (flat paper towel, folded paper towel, shaking off excess water) yield the same results (i.e., students report their hands were completely dry each time), try cutting the paper towel provided down to half its size and retest the variations.
- Alternatively, you could vary the amount of paper towel to emphasize waste. In attempt 1, provide an excessive amount of towel to emphasize waste. In attempt 2, provide a small piece of paper towel, just enough to dry hands. In attempt 3, provide the smaller piece of towel, but have students shake water off their hands and fold the paper towel before drying their hands. Emphasize that any waste produced during this activity will help us save paper in the long run.
- The 5 W's and a How strategy could be used with a text or video as well. Be sure to pose a *How* or *How might* focus question at the start to prompt students to move to solutions and action in the end.

During Language-Arts Time

Use language-arts time to build background knowledge about paper towel waste. Prompt students to revisit their 5 W's and a How questions. Working with a partner or in small groups, students can compile and sort their questions, looking for topics that come up repeatedly. For example, students might notice that they have lots of questions about why paper towels were invented, how they are made, or what environmental problems paper towels cause. Provide time for students to research some of these topics using articles or infographics you provide or via online searches. As a class, revisit the focus question from science class, *How can we rethink or redesign the paper towel to move toward zero waste?* Prompt students to share new ideas they have as a result of their research.

The ABCs of Background Knowledge

Activate, Build, Connect

Properties of Water: Capillary action is the ability of a liquid to flow into narrow spaces without the assistance of any force, because of properties like cohesion, adhesion, and surface tension.

- By folding the paper towel, you create spaces between the layers to hold water.

Vocabulary Spotlight

Hierarchy

- From Greek *hieros* meaning "supernatural" and *archos* meaning "ruler"
- It describes a system that organizes or ranks people or things, often according to power or importance; e.g., Zero Waste Hierarchy
- Related words: hierarchical

5 W's and a How: Better Paper Towel Activity

How can we rethink or redesign the paper towel?

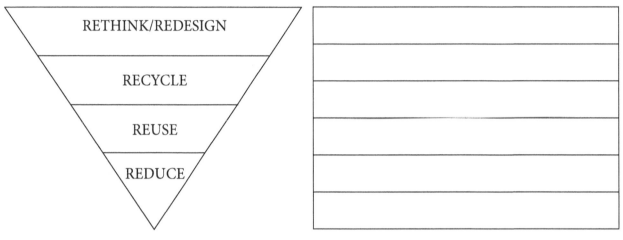

The Zero Waste Hierarchy

RETHINK/REDESIGN

RECYCLE

REUSE

REDUCE

Adapted from: Zero Waste International Alliance

My 5 W's and How Questions

Tracking Our Results from the Better Paper Towel Activity

Use the line below to indicate how your hands feel after each hand-drying attempt.

Attempt 1:   Use the flat paper towel.

Attempt 2:   Use a folded paper towel.

Attempt 3   Shake your hands a few times to remove most of the water and then use a folded paper towel.

Completely Dry   Somewhat Dry   Still Wet

How can we rethink or redesign the paper towel to move toward Zero Waste?

Pembroke Publishers ©2023 *Fail-Safe Strategies for Science and Literacy* by Sandra Mirabelli and Lionel Sandner ISBN 978-1-55138-364-4

Better Paper Towel

Summary

This activity shows how folding paper towels makes them more absorbent, as water molecules are captured between the layers of one piece of paper towel. The activity is then extended in two directions: first, as an estimation activity, for which students determine how much of the paper towel is wet; and second, as a reflection activity, as they consider how much paper towel can be saved using this method of hand-drying.

Hints

- The Ted Talk at https://youtu.be/2FMBSblpcrc is a good resource.
- Brown paper towel works best.

Explanation

By folding the paper towel into four layers, interstitial spaces are created to capture the water between the paper towel's layers. This makes a smaller, but thicker piece of paper towel and more absorbent.

Supplies

- access to water
- paper towels

Directions

1. Wash your hands at the sink. Dry your hands with one paper towel. How well does it dry your hands?
2. Wash your hands again. Dry your hands with one piece of paper towel folded in half twice. Does this dry your hands completely?
3. Wash your hands again. Shake your hands 7 to 12 times to remove the large droplets of water before drying with a folded paper towel.
4. Unfold the wet paper towel and use a pencil to outline the wet areas before the towel dries. Estimate what percentage of the paper is wet. One method is to cut out the outlined wet areas and compare this amount of paper to the dry paper. Remember this is an approximation and does not have to be exact.
5. Discuss how folding one piece of paper towel is good for the environment.

STRATEGY #24
What If...

Strategy Connections

Thinking Routine: Conclude and Apply

Science Activity: How Do You Know It's Fair?, page 149

When to Use: Before the activity
During the activity

The What If... strategy supports students in thinking critically about cause-and-effect relationships. Using this strategy prompts students to look for new solutions and ways to do things differently. In science, this strategy offers an opportunity to work on the skill of identifying and manipulating variables, and on the concept of a fair test. It prompts students to consider how a variable can be changed and what effect this would have on the outcome of an activity or investigation. The What If... strategy engages students in inquiry, as they consider the possibilities of changing one variable.

Using the Strategy with the How Do You Know It's Fair? Activity

During Science Time

- As the How Do You Know it's Fair? activity on page 149 is being introduced, invite students to identify things that would have to be the same or be controlled in each group so that no one has an unfair advantage when trying for a slow dissolving rate. Have students record these variables on the What If... strategy organizer on page 148 in the first section, 1. Control Variables. Students might offer such variables as *the type of candy, the size of the candy, where the candy is held in a person's mouth.*

- Once the activity is complete, have students record the time it took to dissolve the candy in the appropriate box in the Measure Time section. They should share this information with the class.

- Ask students to consider how they could speed up the time it takes to dissolve the candy. Refer them back to the Control Variables they identified. Is there a variable listed there that could be altered in some way to speed up the dissolving of the candy? Encourage students to record several options in the What If... boxes on the strategy organizer. For example,

    What if we hold the candy under our tongue?
    What if we move the candy around in our mouth?
    What if we hold it against the roof of our mouth?
    What if we drink something warm before placing the candy in our mouth?

- Finally, have each group discuss which of their What If... options is most likely to result in the candy dissolving faster. Be sure to discuss that, in order to be a fair test, only one variable can be changed, so that you can see the effect of that change on time. Allow students to formulate a new question to investigate by completing the *If... Then... Because...* sentence stem at the bottom of the strategy organizer.

Variations/Tips/Useful Prompts

- When they are looking at how to manipulate a variable, students can consider varying the physical properties of the substance, such as the size, the temperature, or the amount of the substance as a starting point.

- Consider having students expand their What If... statements to develop a scientific hypothesis, or an idea about a phenomenon that can be tested or observed and possibly found to be incorrect. To support students in doing this, use the sentence stem *If... Then ... Because....* This sentence stem asks students to connect their hypothesis to scientific reasoning by explaining what prior knowledge or evidence led them to make their If... Then... statement. For example, in the How Do You Know It's Fair? activity, students might write, *If we break down the size of the candy into smaller pieces, then the candy will dissolve more quickly, because there will be more surface area in contact with our saliva to help it dissolve faster.*

During Language-Arts Time

- Consider using language-arts time to help students build a better understanding of the scientific concepts of *melting* and *dissolving*. Remind students that, when you did the Candy Color Wheel activity (page 70), you talked about chocolate melting (one substance that is the same in solid or liquid state when heat is added). However when working with hard candy (a solution made of several substances), you will talk about dissolving. Students might offer that using the Frayer Model strategy #20 (page 132) might be a useful way to build knowledge about and distinguish between these two terms.
- Students can build background knowledge by researching various factors that affect dissolving rates and why this might be relevant in real life. For example, knowing how different substances dissolve in different environments can help students understand things like why it's important to take certain medications with food so that they're absorbed by the body, or why certain drinks are made with hot or cold water. The more students read, research, and experiment with solubility, the more they'll see the many applications it can have in our lives.

The ABCs of Background Knowledge *Activate, Build, Connect*	Vocabulary Spotlight
Dissolving: the process by which a solute (e.g., sugar) forms a solution with another substance, the solvent (e.g., water) - A candy dissolves in your mouth because the sugar (the solute) combines with the saliva (the solvent) to create a sugar solution.	*Variables* - From Latin *varius* meaning "different, varies, can change"; suffix *–able* means "capable of; able to be" - Related words: vary, various

What If…: How Do You Know It's Fair?

We know it's fair because we…

1. Control Variables
What must be the same or controlled to ensure that each group is conducting a fair test and no one has an unfair advantage?

2. Measure Time (the dependent variable) to compare your results to others' results.
What will you measure in order to be able to compare results from different groups conducting the same test?

How long did it take for your group's candy to dissolve?

Think about how we can dissolve the candy at a faster rate. Complete the What if… stems to record your ideas:

What if _____

What if _____

What if _____

Our New Fair Test

If we _____

Then _____

Because _____

_____

Pembroke Publishers ©2023 *Fail-Safe Strategies for Science and Literacy* by Sandra Mirabelli and Lionel Sandner ISBN 978-1-55138-364-4

How Do You Know It's Fair?

Summary

Students create a fair test to determine the fastest rate for dissolving a hard candy in their mouths. The concept of a fair test, when only one variable in an experiment is changed, is important for students to develop and understand. This activity provides the motivation of candy and a focus on developing a fair test by identifying and controlling as many variables as possible.

Hints

Students might confuse melting and dissolving. Melting is a phase change that requires the addition of heat; for example, melting chocolate in your mouth. Dissolving involves two substances that result in a solution; for example, a sugar-based candy dissolving in the saliva in your mouth.

Explanation

A fair test is a process for answering a question by controlling all the variables except one. How that one variable changes provides evidence for answering the question. By repeating the fair test and collecting multiple results, conclusions that answer the question can be drawn from the evidence.

In this activity, the variable students are testing, also called the independent or manipulated variable, is the condition of the candy in their mouth; the dependent or responding variable is the time it takes the candy to dissolve; all other variables that are not to be changed are called the controlled variables. Examples of controlled variables include placement of candy on tongue, no chewing, and mouth closed.

Supplies

- hard candy (ideally one that takes 2–4 minutes to dissolve)
- timing device

Directions

1. Put a candy in your mouth and time how long it takes for the candy to dissolve. Record class results.
2. In groups, identify variables that can be controlled so that the timing of the rate of dissolving can be as fair as possible.
3. With your group, create your own fair test.
4. Take a candy to perform your fair test and record your results.

STRATEGY #25
What? So What? Now What?

The What? So What? Now What? strategy (adapted from Rolfe et al., 2001) engages students in reflective thinking after an experience. The strategy has three phases: first, students are prompted to identify what happened; second, they consider the implications and importance of these results; and finally, they engage in forward thinking about how this new knowledge might be applied as a solution to a problem.

Using this Strategy with the Iodine Clock Activity

During Science Time

- Provide students with the opportunity to record the **What?** or what they noticed in the Iodine Clock activity on page 153, using the space provided on the What? So What? Now What? Iodine Clock strategy organizer on page 152. Let students know that documenting observations that include how the materials changed during the activity would be appropriate in this stage of the strategy; for example, students might comment on the color change or the rate of the change.
- Next, have students consider the **So What?** You might want to further support students by having them consider the following: *Did anything surprising or unexpected happen? Was there a pattern to what happened? Why is this important?*
- Finally, have students consider the **Now What?** phase of the strategy. Prompt students to use the third box on the strategy organizer to record what they learned about rates of reaction in this activity by considering the changes to the materials. Then have them list wonderings they have about this reaction. Invite students to choose a researchable wondering (see Strategy #11 Question Sorter on page 93) and ask them how this wondering might help in another situation; e.g., medicine, the environment, consumer product design.

Variations/Tips/Useful Prompts
- The What? So What? Now What? strategy can also be used with a variety of issue-based topics in science. Working through the three phases of the strategy can lead to action-oriented outcomes and help students see that learning in one area of science could be applied to another area and provide insight and possible solutions to existing problems.
- This strategy would be useful for group problem-solving activities as well.

During Language-Arts Time

Have students work with the What? So What? Now What? strategy to consider the concept of time in science and across other subject areas.

- Start by posting the following riddle: **What** *has a beginning but no end, has a start but no finish, and is always running forward, never back?* Encourage students to relate each part of the riddle to their proposed answer. The answer to this riddle is *time*.

- After some discussion of how each part of the riddle relates to time, proceed to the **So What?** part of the strategy by posting samples of different ways we use and look at time across various subject areas. For example, you could post

  - a time signature on a music staff
  - a visual of Salvador Dali's Persistence of Memory painting
  - the formula in science for velocity (v = distance/time)
  - a road sign displaying speed in km/h or miles/h
  - a graph in math with time along the x axis
  - a sentence that portrays the literary technique of foreshadowing; e.g., "I have a bad feeling about this," spoken by Han Solo in *Star Wars*

  Prompt students to identify the different subject areas where we might encounter these different ways to use and portray time, and why it is important in each field. The examples can provide further support if students haven't already solved the opening riddle. Then ask students to consider tools we use to measure time. Students might offer *clocks, stop watches, calendars, their phones.*

- Finally, engage students with the **Now What?** part of the strategy by referring to the Iodine Clock activity and asking students to consider why time is important in scientific research and what it allows us to do. Lead a discussion to help students see that, in many research activities, from astronomy to biology, time is often the dependent variable that we use to measure a change. It allows us to track growth, progress, or the attributes of an object or event so that we can make comparisons.

- For students who would like to continue researching and discussing the concept of time, there are a number of online articles that can be found by searching the topic "What is time?" that can support further thinking and the building of background knowledge.

The ABCs of Background Knowledge *Activate, Build, Connect*	Vocabulary Spotlight
Rates of Reaction: Chemical reactions can be fast or slow. The rate of a reaction can be changed by factors like temperature, concentration, and surface area of materials. • You can make the iodine clock reaction vary in time by changing the temperature of the starting materials.	*Iodine* • From Greek *iod* meaning "violet-colored"; suffix *–ine* is commonly used in chemistry to identify a substance or element • Iodine is represented by the symbol I and has atomic number 53

What? So What? Now What?
Iodine Clock Activity

What happened during this activity? Record your observations below.

So What?

Did anything surprising or unexpected happen during this activity? Did you see any patterns? Why are the results of this activity important?

Now What?

What have you learned about rates of reactions from this activity? What wonderings do you have as a result of this activity? How might this learning help us in another context, situation, or field of science: e.g., medicine, the environment, consumer product design?

Pembroke Publishers ©2023 *Fail-Safe Strategies for Science and Literacy* by Sandra Mirabelli and Lionel Sandner ISBN 978-1-55138-364-4

Iodine Clock

Three cups filled with everyday solutions. Mix them in a specific order. Wait a minute and a cool color change occurs. It's not magic; it's science!

Hints

- Amounts do not have to be exact, but proportions when mixing do.
- Iodine can be from a first-aid kit or purchased.
- Use hydrogen peroxide at 3% concentration.
- Laundry starch can be spray starch.
- Practice this first, and follow all school safety procedures.

Explanation

The iodine clock reaction is a good introduction to how rates of chemical change can vary. By combining the materials in a specific amount and order, two complex chemical reactions take place. The end result is a dramatic change from a clear liquid to a blue liquid.

Supplies

- 5 transparent plastic cups
- marker
- measuring cups, spoons
- distilled or tap water (distilled preferred)
- tincture of iodine (2%)
- hydrogen peroxide (3%)
- liquid laundry starch
- 1000 mg vitamin C tablets

Direction

1. With the marker, label cups A, B, C, and 1, 2.
2. Using Cups A, B, and C, make solutions with the following materials:

   Cup A: Crush two 1000 mg Vitamin C tablets; dissolve in 60 ml/⅓ cup water.
   Cup B: Mix 5 ml/1 teaspoon iodine with 15 ml/1 tablespoon water.
   Cup C: Mix 15 ml/1 tablespoon hydrogen peroxide, 5 ml/1 tablespoon starch, and 15 ml/1 tablespoon water.

2. Using Cups 1 and 2, create the following solutions:

   Cup 1: 5 ml/1 teaspoon from Cup A, 2 ml/½ teaspoon from Cup B, 30 ml/2 tablespoons water
   Cup 2: 30 ml/2 tablespoons from Cup C

3. Pour contents of Cup 1 into Cup 2.
4. Pour contents of Cup 2 back into Cup 1.
5. Observe.

While the exact details of this reaction are not necessary for this activity, a brief explanation would start with pointing out starch will turn dark blue or black when iodine is added. If Vitamin C is present, the iodine will react faster with it than the starch. Once all the Vitamin C has reacted, the iodine will immediately interact with the starch to turn the solution blue.

Safety

Iodine can stain hands and clothing. Take appropriate precautions when using it.

References

Brown, P. C., Roediger, H. L., III, & McDaniel, M. A. (2014). *Make It Stick: The science of successful learning.* Harvard University Press.

Cervetti, G.N., Hiebert, E.H. (2018). "Knowledge at the Center of English/ Language Arts Instruction." *The Reading Teacher 72*(4).

Cervetti, G., Pearson, P. D., Barber, J., Hiebert, E., Bravo, M. (2007). Integrating literacy and science:. In M. Pressley, A. K. Billman, K. Perry, K. Refitt & J. Reynolds (Eds.), *Shaping Literacy Achievement: The research we have, the research we need* (pp. 157–174). New York, NY: The Guilford Press.

Dehaene, S. (2021). *How We Learn: Why Brains Learn Better Than Any Machine... for Now.* New York, NY: Penguin.

Drake, S. M., Reid, J. L., & Kolohon, W., (2014). *Interweaving Curriculum and Classroom Assessment: Engaging the 21st-centurylLearner.* Canada: Oxford University Press.

Duke, N.K., Ward, A.E., & Pearson, P.D. (2021). "The Science of Reading Comprehension Instruction." *The Reading Teacher*, 74(6), 663–672. https:// doi.org/10.1002/trtr.1993

Edutopia. Brain-based Learning. (2014, December 17). https://www.edutopia. org/blog/why-curiosity-enhances-learning-marianne-stenger.

Fang, Z., Lamme, L., & Pringle, R. (2010). *Language and Literacy in Inquiry-based Science Classrooms, Grades 3–8.* Thousand Oaks, CA: Corwin & NSTA Press.

Fang, Z., & Wei, Y. (2010). "Improving middle school students' science literacy through reading infusion." *The Journal of Educational Research, 103*(4), 262–273. https://doi.org/10.1080/00220670903383051

Finson, K. D. (2010). "Inference or Observation?" *Science & Children, 48* (2), 44–47.

Fisher, D. and Frey, N. (2009) *Background Knowledge: The missing piece of the comprehension puzzle.* Portsmouth, NH: Heinemann.

Fisher, D., Frey, N., & Hattie, J. (2016). *Visible Learning for Literacy, Grades K–12.* Thousand Oaks, CA: Corwin.

Fries-Gaither, J., & Shiverdecker, T. (2013). *Inquiring Scientists, Inquiring Readers: Using nonfiction to promote science literacy, grades --5.* Arlington, VA: NSTA Press.

Furst, Efrat. Teaching with learning in mind. https://sites.google.com/view/efratfurst/teaching-with-learning-in-mind?authuser=0

Gladwell, M. (2005). *Blink: The power of thinking without thinking.* New York, NY: Little, Brown and Co.

Hardiman, M. (2012). *The Brain-targeted Teaching Model for 21st-Century Schools.* Thousand Oaks, CA: Corwin.

Hartman, J., Nelson, E. Kirschner, P., (2022). "Improving student success in chemistry through cognitive science." *Foundations of Chemistry* (2022) 24:239–261.

Hattie, J. (2009). *Visible Learning: A synthesis of over 800 meta-analyses relating to achievement.* New York, NY: Routledge.

Howell, E. L. & Brossard, D. (2020). "(Mis)informed about what? What it means to be a science-literate citizen in a digital world." Proceedings of the National Academy of Sciences 118(15):e1912436117 DOI:10.1073/pnas.1912436117

Kahneman, D. (2011). *Thinking Fast and Slow.* Farrar, Straus and Giroux.

Keeley, P. (2016). *Science Formative Assessment, Volume 1: 75 practical strategies for linking assessment, instruction, and learning (2nd edition).* Thousand Oaks, CA: Corwin.

Keeley, P. (2015). *Science Formative Assessment, Volume 2: 50 more strategies for linking assessment, instruction, and learning.* Thousand Oaks, CA: Corwin.

Kirschner, P., & Hendrick, C. (2020). *How Learning Happens: Seminal works in educational psychology and what they mean in practice.* New York, NY: Routledge.

Krajcik, J. (2014). The Importance of Viable Models in the Construction of Professional Development. In Wojnowski, B. S. and Pea, C. H. (eds.), *Models and Approaches to STEM Professional Development.* Arlington: VA: NSTA Press.

Mayer, R. E., & Fiorella, L. (2022). *The Cambridge Handbook of Multimedia Learning.*

Mayer, R. E., & Moreno, R. (2003). "Nine Ways to Reduce Cognitive Load in Multimedia Learning." *Educational Psychologist, 38*(1), 43–52.

Neuman, S. B., Kaefer, T., Pinkham, A. (2014). "Building Background Knowledge." *The Reading Teacher.* 68(2), 145–148.

Neuman, S. B. (2019). "Comprehension in Disguise: The Role of Knowledge in Children's Learning." *Perspectives on Language and Literacy*, 45(4), 12–16. International Dyslexia Association.

Pass, F., & Kirschner, F. (2012) "Goal-Free Effect." *Encyclopedia of the Sciences of Learning*, 1375–1377.

Pearson, P. D., Moje, E., & Greenleaf, C. (2010). "Literacy and Science: Each in the service of the other." *Science, 328*(5977), 459–463.

Reinert, S., Hübener, M., Bonhoeffer, T., & Goltstein, P. M. (2021). "Mouse prefrontal cortex represents learned rules for categorization." *Nature, 593*(7859), 411–417. https://doi.org/10.1038/s41586-021-03452-z

Ritchhart, R., Church, M., & Morrison, K. (2011). *Making Thinking Visible: how to promote engagement, understanding and independence for all learners.* San Francisco, CA: Jossey-Bass.

Ritchhart, R., and Church, M. (2020). *The Power of Making Thinking Visible: Practices to engage and empower all learners.* Hoboken, NJ: Jossey-Bass.

Rolfe, G., Freshwater, D., Jasper, M. (2001) *Critical Reflection in Nursing and the Helping Professions: A user's guide.* London, UK: Palgrave Macmillan.

Senge, P. (2006). *The Fifth Discipline: The art and practice of the learning organization.* New York, NY: Doubleday/Currency.

Shanahan, T. (2023, July 22). Knowledge or Comprehension Strategies: What Should We Teach? Shanahan on Literacy. https://www.shanahanonliteracy.com/blog/knowledge-or-comprehension-strategies-what-should-we-teach

Sharon, Aviv J., & Baram-Tsabari, A. (2020). "Can science literacy help individuals identify misinformation in everyday life?" *Science Education,* 104(5), 873 - 894.

Weinstein, Y., Sumeracki, M., & Caviglioli, O. (2019). *Understanding How We Learn: A Visual Guide.* New York, NY: Routledge.

Wexler, N. (2020). *The Knowledge Gap: The hidden cause of America's broken education system – and how to fix it.* Penguin-Random House: New York.

White, R., & Gunstone, R. (1992). *Probing Understanding (1st ed.).* New York, NY: Routledge. https://doi.org/10.4324/9780203761342

Willingham, D. T. (2006). "How Knowledge Helps: It speeds and strengthens reading comprehension, learning—and thinking." *American Educator,* 30(1), 30–37.

Willingham, D.T., (2017). *The Reading Mind: A cognitive approach to understanding how the mind reads.* San Francisco, CA: Jossey-Bass.

Willingham, D.T. (2021). *Why Don't Students Like School?* San Francisco, CA: Jossey-Bass.

Yore, Larry, Bisanz, Gay L. & Hand, Brian M. (2003) "Examining the literacy component of science literacy: 25 years of language arts and science research." *International Journal of Science Education,* 25:6, 689-725, DOI: 10.1080/09500690305018

Zadina, J. N. (2014). *Multiple Pathways to the Student Brain: Energizing and enhancing instruction.* San Francisco: CA: Jossey-Bass.

Zero Waste International Alliance (2022). The Zero Waste Hierarchy, Version 8.0. Retrieved from: https://zwia.org/zwh/ .

Zikes, D. (2008). *Math Connects, Grades PK–5: Dinah Zike's teaching math & science with foldables.* New York, NY: McGraw-Hill Education.

Index